TERROR, TERRORISM, AND THE HUMAN CONDITION

Series Editor: Charles P. Webel

Terror, Terrorism, and the Human Condition by Charles P. Webel

TERROR, TERRORISM, AND THE HUMAN CONDITION

Charles P. Webel

First published 2004 by
PALGRAVE MACMILLAN™
175 Fifth Avenue, New York, N.Y. 10010 and
Houndmills, Basingstoke, Hampshire, England RG21 6XS
Companies and representatives throughout the world.

PALGRAVE MACMILLAN is the global academic imprint of the Palgrave Macmillan division of St. Martin's Press, LLC and of Palgrave Macmillan Ltd. Macmillan® is a registered trademark in the United States, United Kingdom and other countries. Palgrave is a registered trademark in the European Union and other countries.

ISBN 1–4039–6161–1 hardback

Library of Congress Cataloging-in-Publication Data

Webel, Charles.
    Terrror, terrorism, and the human condition / Charles P. Webel.
        p. cm.
    Includes bibliographical references and index.
    ISBN 1–4039–6161–1
      1. Terrorism. 2. Terrorism—History. 3. Terror. 4. Victims of terrrorism.
    5. Pacifism. 6. Peaceful change (International relations) I. Title.

HV6431.W42 2004
303.6′25—dc22   2004049006

A catalogue record for this book is available from the British Library.

Design by Newgen Imaging Systems (P) Ltd., Chennai, India.

First edition: November 2004

10 9 8 7 6 5 4 3 2 1

Printed in the United States of America.

Contents

ACKNOWLEDGMENTS

My acknowledgments are legion. First, I wish to thank the 52 survivors of terrifying political attacks who graciously gave me their time and opened their souls. Without their cooperation, this book would not be possible. Next, I wish to express my gratitude to the German-American Fulbright Commission, which provided me with a grant enabling me to travel to Germany and conduct interviews in Europe. I also wish to acknowledge the graciousness and support of the Anglistisches Seminar of the University of Heidelberg, as well as to Professor Dieter Schulz, Dr. Bernhard Kuhn, and Mr. Jakob Köllhofer, all in Heidelberg. I would also like to thank the global peace organization TRANSCEND, which facilitated my fieldwork by posting my web announcements looking for volunteers.

Next, I wish to acknowledge the many people who served as interpreters during my interviews with terrorism survivors and who provided other kinds of equally indispensable support in their respective countries. In particular, I am deeply grateful to Larisa Stanijauska in Latvia and Japan; Elena Mikhalina and Adriy Kravets in Ukraine; Maryann Shoemaker and Alina Kravchenko in Russia; Ulla Timmerman in Denmark; Jaro Sveceny in the Czech Republic; James Wills, Rupert Read, and Marlon Schwarz in England; Eduardo Flores and the Association for the Victims of Terrorism (AVT) in Spain; Diana van Bergen in Holland; Cecilia Taiana in Canada; and Timothy O'Connor, Peggy Rafferty, and Jean Maria Arrigo in the United States.

It is to the past, present, and future victims of terrorism—in all its deadly manifestations—that I dedicate this book.

Introduction

Pondering the Imponderable

Hourly afflict: merely, thou art death's fool;
What's yet in this
That bears the name of life
Lie hid moe thousand deaths: yet we fear,
That makes these odds all even . . . .
To sue to live, I find I seek to die:
And, seeking death, find life: let it come on . . . .
The sense of death is most in apprehension;
Ay, but to die, and go we know not where: . . .
The weariest and most loathed worldly life
That age, ache, penury, and imprisonment
Can lay on nature is a paradise
To what we fear of death.

Shakespeare, *Measure for Measure*, Act III, i.

Our war against terror is only beginning.

President George W. Bush

This is not just a question of fighting terrorism . . . . This is a milestone in history, like Hitler and Napoleon. What we're finding is that there can't be economic globalization without human and spiritual globalization. We have to look for the causes of things. If you assume that human beings are not totally bad in themselves, then something must have gone terribly wrong.

Christoph von Dohnanyi

Surely it is time, half a century after Hiroshima, to embrace a universal morality, to think of all children, everywhere, as our own.

Howard Zinn

Terror is a six-letter word. So is murder.

Terror and murder are among the most vexing words in our lexicon; they are also among the most distressing features of the human condition.

Terror, terrorism, and murder are notoriously difficult to define, discomforting to contemplate, and anguishing to experience or behold. And although terror, terrorism, and murder are existentially, psychologically, and historically linked, their affinities have seldom been noted, much less scrutinized.

But the lives and fates of each one of us, of our species as a whole, indeed of life on Earth itself, may depend on humanity's collective ability, or inability, to come to terms with terror, terrorism, and murder (often taken to be synonymous with "*un*justified" and/or "unlawful" killing). Given the current series of terrifying attacks and counterattacks on a global scale, it is possible that this escalating and spreading cycle of violence ("terrorism and counterterrorism") may spiral out of control—and may soon include the use of weapons of mass destruction (by multiple agents?). It is therefore imperative that we understand the roots of terror—as well as the reasons for terrorism (and counterterrorism)—and then take informed actions to reduce the mortal threat to our existence, as well as to all life on Earth, posed by these weapons and the people who would (and will?) deploy them.

Initially, we must attempt to understand how and why we feel terrified, and under which circumstances many of us wish (need?) to kill, and to justify killing, one another. Then, we ought to see if these feelings, thoughts, and desires are malleable and controllable—possibly unlike "The Human Condition," which constitutes the background against which terror and murder all too often take center stage The human condition is what makes it possible for us to be human. It is also our collective "fate," and is not (or at least not yet) under our control. Is it possible (or likely...) that terror, terrorism, and murder may *to some degree be regulated, even reduced, if not completely eliminated*? If so, how and when? If not, why not?

There may or may not be reassuring answers to these questions, which are among the most pressing of our time, of our history. But it is imperative that they be raised and addressed, even if the "answers" are disquieting.

This book is a multidimensional exploration of terror, terrorism, and the human condition. It is an attempt to demystify our now centuries-long attraction to, and dread of, terror and its progeny, including terrorism (or political terror) and (mass) murder. It is also a call to thought, and an appeal to reasoned action.

Terror, Terrorism, and the Human Condition is a book that may well raise more issues than it resolves. At the dawn of this new millennium, this is absolutely necessary if we are to understand our "nature" and history. But it is not sufficient. If we hope to diminish and eventually eliminate the danger to our planet posed by two existential threats to the Earth, both with the acronyms WMD—namely Weapons of Mass Destruction and Writings of Mass Deception—we must move beyond thinking and writing to doing and renewing.

A "war on terror," like a "war on drugs," cannot be won and must not be fought any further. For "war" cannot possibly succeed in eliminating terror from our human condition—or even "defeat" myriads of "terrorists and the states that harbor them"—any more than laws and prisons have "succeeded" in uprooting the cravings of millions of people to alter their moods and minds by taking drugs (ranging from alcohol and tobacco to sedatives, hallucinogenics, and hypnotics).

But this does *not* imply that "terror and terrorism" cannot, and should not, be confronted by means *other than* war(s) and by strategies that eschew, if not completely eliminate, other forms of state and non-state violence. For there may well be more effective and humane ways of managing terror—and of effectively dealing with "terrorism and terrorists"—than war and other forms of state—sanctioned violence (often resulting in mass murder).

In fact, there may well already exist nonviolent and socially appropriate means of action and political intervention that are at least as "effective" (or no more "ineffective")—and are certainly less lethal and therefore more ethical—in addressing the roots of terror and in reducing acts of terrorist (and counterterrorist) violence than bombing and assassinating "terrorists and those who harbor them." If we are to survive, we may also need to create new, basically nonviolent, means to resolve conflicts and to reduce their lethality.

Terror, Terrorism, and the Human Condition is possibly a paradoxical endeavor. It is a linguistic inquiry into a nonverbal realm, namely, the murky depths of human souls wracked by unbearable feelings of intense existential anguish, aka "terror." It is also an effort to ponder the imponderable—the possible (probable?) end of our species, and not in the distant future. To think the "unthinkable" (extinction), to make sense of what may be inexplicable (the roots of terror and the reasons for terrorism) and to change the (possibly) unchangeable (the human condition)—these may well be quixotic undertakings. But they are necessary, if paradoxical, projects, at least for me. Let us begin to ponder the imponderable.

1

DEFINING THE INDEFINABLE: WHAT ARE, AND ARE NOT "TERROR, TERRORISM, AND THE HUMAN CONDITION?"

THE SETTING

On September 11, 2001, during the first year of this new millennium, the cities of New York and Washington D.C. were attacked by terrorists with radical Islamist ties. The loss of life—approximately 3,000 civilians—was exceeded in American history only by battles during the Civil War, although cities in other countries had far greater civilian casualties during World War II.

Exactly 911 days later, on March 11, 2004, commuter trains in Madrid, Spain, were bombed by terrorists with presumed radical Islamist links. Almost 200 people were killed and more than 1,400 injured. This was the greatest single-day loss of life due to a terrorist attack on a Western European country. Three days after this attack, the conservative Spanish government—which, in the face of mass popular opposition, supported the United States' invasion and occupation of Iraq—was defeated in a general election it had been expected to win. It was replaced by a Socialist administration pledged to withdraw Spanish forces from Iraq.

A number of factors make the events of September 11, 2001 and their aftermath unprecedented in American history: First, the attacks were perpetrated by foreign terrorists on American soil. Second, U.S. civilian airplanes were transformed into weapons of mass destruction. Third, the United States was not in a declared state of war at the time. Fourth, the identities of the perpetrators were unknown at the time and were probably "non-state actors." Fifth, a weapon of bio-terrorism, anthrax, was subsequently used against Americans on American soil. Sixth, millions of Americans, as well as many civilians in other countries, have felt unprecedented levels of stress, anxiety, trauma, and related feelings of having been "terrorized" by these attacks. Finally, no one has claimed direct responsibility for the events of 9/11, in contrast to most other terrorist attacks and acts of violence committed against civilian populations during wartime and since 1945.[1]

According to a study conducted by the Rand corporation and published in the November 15, 2001 issue of *The New England Journal of Medicine* (*NEJM*),[2] 90 percent of the people surveyed reported they had experienced at least some degree of stress three to five days after the initial attacks on 9/11, while 44 percent were trying to cope with "substantial symptoms." These symptoms include the respondents' feeling "very upset" when they were reminded of what happened on 9/11; repeated, disturbing memories, thoughts, and/or dreams; difficulty concentrating; trouble falling and/or staying asleep; and feelings of anger and/or angry outbursts. Furthermore, the Rand study found that 47 percent of interviewed parents reported that their children were worried about their own safety and/or the safety of loved ones, and that 35 percent of the respondents' children had one or more clear symptoms of stress. The survey concluded with a list of measures taken by these randomly selected American adults to cope with their feelings of anxiety and stress.

A number of subsequent studies have corroborated and extended these findings. Another article in the *NEJM*[3] found that in Manhattan, five to eight weeks after the September 11 attacks, 7.5 percent of surveyed adults reported symptoms consistent with a diagnosis of Post Traumatic Stress Disorder (PTSD), almost 10 percent seemed currently depressed, and among respondents who lived near the World Trade Center (WTC), the prevalence of PTSD was 20 percent. Interestingly, this study indicated that one of the strongest predictors of PTSD was Hispanic ethnicity—a fascinating finding, one consistent with previous psychiatric investigations of PTSD among Hispanic Vietnam War veterans, and a matter I will take up in my discussion and analysis of the interviews I conducted.[4]

Other studies have found that the terrorist attacks of 9/11 constituted an "unprecedented exposure to trauma in the United States" (though the extent and degree of possible trauma differ somewhat, depending on the particular study). One study—called "Psychological Reactions to Terrorist Attacks" and published in the *Journal of the*

American Medical Association (*JAMA*)—found that one–two months after those attacks, the prevalence of probable PTSD was significantly higher in the New York City metropolitan areas (11.2 percent) than in Washington D.C. (only 2.7 percent, perhaps surprisingly low, given the attack on the Pentagon) and in the rest of the United States (about 4 percent).[5] Another study published in *JAMA* found that 17 percent of the U.S. population outside New York reported PTSD-like symptoms two months after 9/11, and 5.6 percent did so six months after the attacks. The highest levels of PTSD symptoms were associated with gender (women were 1.64 times as likely as men to have PTSD), marital separation, pre–September 11 depression and/or anxiety disorder, physical illness, severity of exposure to the attacks, and/or early abandonment of coping efforts (such as giving up, denial, and/or self-distraction).[6]

In Spain and some other advanced industrial societies (especially Israel), terrorist attacks, counterterrorist operations, and public awareness about the dangers of terrorism and counterterrorism are decades-old. As a result of strenuous efforts by Spanish survivors of terrorist (mainly by ETA, a violent Basque separatist group) attacks, a support system has been developed in Spain to provide terror victims with counseling, psychotherapy, and other needed services. The level of PTSD among Spanish terror victims—especially women—seems very high, even when compared with New York after September 11. And the March 11 attack on Madrid commuters is certain to increase the preexisting vulnerability of many Spaniards to PTSD.

How generalizable are these findings? How long will people feel this way, even in the unlikely event that no significant additional acts of terrorist violence are perpetrated on North American or European soil? And how will everyday citizens and policy-makers behave if there are more events like September 11, 2001, and March 11, 2004?

How might we try to account for the usage of "terrorism" as a political tactic and of terror as a predictable human response to the violence, and threats of violence, employed by terrorists against innocent people? And w*hat* might we all learn about terror from the experiences of people around the world who underwent and survived terrifying acts of political violence during the twentieth century? These are the questions that orient my multidisciplinary investigation of terror, terrorism, and the human condition.

To begin to address these and related questions, it is necessary (if somewhat perilous, given the absence of consensus regarding these matters) to define some crucial terms. First, I explore "terrorism."

What is "Terrorism?"

"The term 'terrorism' means premeditated, politically motivated violence perpetrated against noncombatant targets by subnational groups or clandestine agents, usually intended to influence an audience."[7]

Central Intelligence Agency

...it (terrorism) is distinguished from all other kinds of violence by its "bifocal" character; namely, by the fact that the immediate acts of terrorist violence, such as shootings, bombings, kidnappings, and hostage-taking, are intended as means to certain goals..., which vary with the particular terrorist acts or series of such acts...the concept of terrorism is a "family resemblance" concept....Consequently, the concept as a whole is an "open" or "open-textured" concept, nonsharply demarcated from other types/forms of individual or collective violence. The major types of terrorism are: predatory, retaliatory, political, and political–moralistic/religious. The terrorism may be domestic or international, "from above"—that is, state or state-sponsored terrorism, or "from below."[8]

Haig Khatchadourian

...terrorism is fundamentally a form of psychological warfare. Terrorism is designed, as it has always been, to have profound psychological repercussions on a target audience. Fear and intimidation are precisely the terrorists' timeless stock-in-trade....It is used to create unbridled fear, dark insecurity, and reverberating panic. Terrorists seek to elicit an irrational, emotional response.[9]

Bruce Hoffman

Etymologically, "terrorism" derives from "terror." Originally the word meant a system, or regime, of terror: at first imposed by the Jacobins, who applied the word to themselves without any negative connotations; subsequently it came to be applied to any policy or regime of the sort and to suggest a strongly negative attitude, as it generally does today....Terrorism is meant to cause terror (extreme fear) and, when successful, does so. Terrorism is intimidation with a purpose: the terror is meant to cause others to do things they would otherwise not do. Terrorism is coercive intimidation.[10]

Igor Primoratz

In searching for a universal definition of "terrorism," a concept that is as contested ("one man's terrorist is another man's freedom fighter ...") as it is "open," I found that "terrorism" has been used most often to denote politically motivated attacks by *subnational* agents (this part is virtually uncontested in the relevant scholarly literature) *and/or states* (this is widely debated, but increasingly accepted outside the United States) on *non*combatants, usually in the context of war, revolution, and struggles for national liberation. In this sense, "terrorism" is as old as violent human conflict.

However, "terrorism," and "terrorists" have become relativized in recent times, since there is very little consensus on who, precisely, is, or is not, a "terrorist," or what is, or is not, an act of "terrorism." Thus, who is or is not a "terrorist," and what may or may not be "acts of terrorism," depend largely on the perspective of the group or the person using (or abusing) those terms.[11]

"Terrorism" is clearly a subcategory of political violence in particular, and of violence in general. Almost all current definitions of terrorism known to me focus on the violent *acts* committed (or threatened) by "terrorists," and neglect *the effects of those acts on their victims*. My focus is on the *terrifying effects* of certain violent acts on the victims of those acts, rather than on continuing the never-ending debate as to who is, or is not, a "terrorist." Nonetheless, for functional purposes, following Khatchadourian, Hoffman, and Johan Galtung,[12] I propose the following definition of "terrorism:"

Terrorism is a premeditated, usually politically motivated, use, or threatened use, of violence, in order to induce a state of terror in its immediate victims, usually for the purpose of influencing another, less reachable audience, such as a government.

Note that under this definition, *both* nation-states—which commit "*terrorism from above*" (TFA)—*and* subnational entities (individuals and groups alike)—which engage in "*terrorism from below*" (TFB)— may commit acts of terrorism. Note as well, that the somewhat artificial, but conventionally accepted, distinction between "combatants" and "noncombatants" does not come into play here. This conceptualization distinguishes my understanding of terrorism from the "official" one of the U.S. government, and from that of many, but not all, writers on this topic. It also distinguishes *political* terrorism—the focus of this book and of virtually all research known to me—from other forms of terrorism, especially *criminal* terrorism.[13]

In agreement with the philosopher Jürgen Habermas and the linguist/social critic Noam Chomsky, I am also claiming that "terrorism" is a *political construct*, a historically variable and ideologically useful way of branding those who may violently oppose a particular policy or government as beyond the moral pale, and hence "not worthy" of diplomacy and negotiations.[14] Moreover, yesterday's "terrorists" may become today's or tomorrow's chief(s) of state—if they are successful in seizing or gaining state power (historical examples abound, from the "barbarian" Teutonic insurgents who overthrew the Roman

Empire, to the Jacobins during early days of the French Revolution, and more recently, the Jewish terrorists in Irgun who were among the founders of the state of Israel). After accession to state power, the victors often (re)write the history books to (re)label themselves as "freedom fighters" "patriots," and/or proponents of "national liberation," and to denote their vanquished adversaries as "terrorists," "autocrats," "imperialists," and so on.

Following Habermas's line of argument, terrorism therefore acquires its political content *retrospectively*, based on the success (see the above examples) or failure (al-Qaeda so far) of those who employ political violence in achieving specific political goals (anti-imperialism, revolutionary insurrection, nation-building, and/or radical Islamic jihad, etc.). Many politically powerful contemporary opponents of "terrorism" arrogate to themselves a kind of moral superiority, an "ethical high ground" that permits and justifies virtually *any* means (designated "counterterrorism" and/or "preemptive war")—including bombings that result in many civilian casualties ("collateral damage")—to win "the war against terror/ism." But as we will see, this often precipitates a constantly escalating series of attacks and counterattacks, a "cycle of violence," that has global, and potentially omnicidal, implications.

In contrast with the contested term "terrorism," which has perhaps too many definitions and debates, "terror" and "the human condition" are remarkably un(der)defined and unanalyzed.

WHAT IS "TERROR?"

> The idea that you can purchase security from terror by saying nothing about terror is not only morally bankrupt but it is also inaccurate.
>   Australian Prime Minister John Howard

Unfortunately, despite the Australian Prime Minister's assertion, virtually no one has talked in a meaningful way about the root of terrorism—terror. This is an omission that stands out amidst the endless talk of fighting a "war against terrorism/terror." It is also a glaring lacuna in current scholarly investigations (at least in such major Western languages as English, German, and French), which focus *either* on trauma (and Post-Traumatic Stress Disorder, PTSD), *or* on terrorism as a policy problem.

To initiate a broad-based, multidisciplinary inquiry into terror and its "family resemblances," I offer the following provisional definition:

The term "terror" denotes both a phenomenological experience of paralyzing, overwhelming, and ineffable mental anguish, as well as a behavioral response to a real or perceived life-threatening danger.

Terror is profoundly sensory (often auditory), and is pre- or post-verbal. The ineffability of terror is a complement to, and often a result of, the unspeakable horror(s) of war(s) and other forms of collective political violence.

THE HUMAN CONDITION

Finally, terror and terrorism do not occur within an existential and historical vacuum. On the contrary, they are embedded within our common human condition. This is a concept that is as under—defined and unanalyzed as "terror."[15]

In reviewing the available literature, I found that the few books in English that purport to have something to say about "the human condition," are mostly by philosophers and/or theologians working from a "Continental" (German/French) tradition.[16] They tend to be existentialist and/or phenomenological in orientation. This is consistent with the approach I am taking in this book.

Following the political philosopher Hannah Arendt, I provisionally define *the human condition as the sum total of earthly circumstances that make possible the form of species life we call "human."* As Arendt says, "The earth is the very quintessence of the human condition, and earthly nature, for all we know, may be unique in the universe in providing human beings with a habitat in which we can move and breathe without effort and without artifice. The human artifice of the world separates human existence from all mere animal environment, but life itself is outside this artificial world, and through life man remains related to all other living organisms."[17] Arendt also claims that there are three human activities—labor, work, and action— "fundamental" to our condition, and, further, that these activities are "intimately connected with the most general condition of human existence: birth and death, natality and mortality. . . . Human existence is conditioned existence, it would be impossible without things, and things would be a heap of unrelated articles, a non-world, if they were not the conditioners of human existence."[18]

Like most other European commentators on the human condition, Arendt focuses on the "worldliness" of our existence, as well as on our mortality: "Imbedded in a cosmos where everything was immortal, mortality became the hallmark of human existence. . . . The mortality of men lies in the fact that individual life, with a recognizable life-story from birth to death, rises out of biological life. . . . This is mortality: to move along a rectilinear line in a universe where everything, if it moves at all, moves in a cyclical order."[19]

As important as Arendt's book may be, it is not a systematic or comprehensive account of the human condition, or even of "human existence" (a term, like "human reality," often used by other, even more existentially oriented thinkers). There *is no* such general account of the human condition *per se*, unless one regards works like Heidegger's *Being and Time*, Sartre's *Being and Nothingness*, and Merleau-Ponty's *Phenomenology of Perception* as centered on the analysis of the human condition broadly conceived.

Also, while Arendt appropriately signifies mortality as "the" (a?) "hallmark of human existence," she omits the psychological/emotional dimensions of mortality—our anxiety and fears in the face of death/dying as well as our "rebellion" against this terminal terrestrial (cosmic?) condition.

In contrast, the great French existentialist writer Albert Camus, in *The Rebel* and *The Myth of Sisyphus*, "obstinately confronts a world condemned to death and the impenetrable obscurity of the human condition with his demand for life and absolute clarity."[20] Camus laments and protests our condition (what his peer and sometime opponent Jean-Paul Sartre called "human reality" or our "situation"), which constitutes the human element within an "absurd creation."[21] And the German theologian Paul Tillich devotes much of his great book *The Courage to Be* to a vivid description of anxiety, which in his view is rooted in our fear of death, of "ultimate nonbeing." According to Tillich, "... in the anxiety about any special situation anxiety about the human situation as such is implied."[22] Tillich appropriately distinguishes between this "existential" (or "basic") "anxiety," "which is given with human existence itself," and "pathological anxiety," rooted in the "neurotic personalities" so acutely analyzed by Freud and his successors.[23]

Unlike many other existential/phenomenological commentators on our condition, Tillich wrote from a theological (albeit unorthodox) perspective. This is of considerable importance, for if one has "faith" in (the existence/omnipotence of) God and the immortality of the individual human "soul," one's perspective on our existence on Earth may differ significantly from "atheistic," "agnostic," and "deistic" accounts.

For example, Thomas Keating, former abbot of a Trappist monastery, in his book *The Human Condition*, declares: "This is the human condition—to be without the true source of happiness, which is the experience of God, and to have lost the key to happiness, which is the contemplative dimension of life, the path to the increasing assimilation and enjoyment of God's presence.... The chief characteristic of the human condition is that everybody is looking for this key and nobody knows where to find it. The human condition is thus poignant in the extreme."[24]

TERROR, TERRORISM, AND THE HUMAN CONDITION

The "poignancy" of our condition is intensified if one lives ("courageously," following Tillich, or "without appeal," in Camus's terms) in a world that is not just haunted by universal death but wracked by violent conflict. Terror, like mortality, may or may not be an "existential given," something without which we would not be human, or would be less human than we are. (This will be discussed later in this book.) But terror-ism is something humankind has created, not found, on Earth. As such, perhaps it might be "un"-created.

If we do not learn to unmake our own deadly fabrications, our existence, and all life on Earth, may terminate—abruptly and in the not-so-distant future. As Arendt says, " . . . there is no reason to doubt our present ability to destroy all organic life on earth. The question is only whether we wish to use our new scientific and technical knowledge in this direction, and this question cannot be decided by scientific means; it is a political question of the first order and therefore cannot be left to the decision of professional scientists or professional politicians."[25]

It is to perhaps the most pressing political question of our time (of any time?)—terrorism and what to do about it—that I now turn.

2

Depicting the Indescribable:
A Brief History of Terrorism

(With Charles Lindholm)

All wars are terrorism.

Political Slogan

Terrorism is a violent phenomenon and it is probably no mere coincidence that it should give rise to violent emotions, such as anger, irritation, and aggression, and that this should cloud judgment. Nor is the confusion surrounding it all new. Terrorism has long exercised a great fascination, especially at a safe distance. . . . Terrorists have found admirers and publicity agents in all ages. . . . The difficulty with terrorism is that there is no terrorism per se, except perhaps at the abstract level, but different terrorisms. . . . Most authors agree that terrorism is the use or the threat of the use of violence, a method of combat, or a strategy to achieve certain targets, that it aims to induce a state of fear in the victim, that it is ruthless and does not conform with humanitarian rules, and that publicity is an essential factor in the terrorist strategy. Beyond this point definitions diverge, often sharply.[1]

Walter Laqueur

Warfare against civilians, whether inspired by hatred, revenge, greed, or political and psychological insecurity, has been one of the most ultimately self-defeating tactics in military history . . . : the nation or faction that resorts to warfare against civilians most quickly, most often, and most viciously is the nation or faction most likely to see its interests frustrated and, in many cases, its existence terminated . . . : warfare against civilians must never be answered in kind. For as failed a tactic as such warfare has been, reprisals similarly directed at civilians have been even more so—particularly when they have exceeded the original assault in scope.[2]

Caleb Carr

Any written "history" of a phenomenon as controversial and anxiety-provoking as "terrorism"[3] is bound to be selective and somewhat subjective. Because there is little consensus (at least in much of the English-speaking world at this time) regarding terrorism, and due to the potentially enormous number of "terrorist" incidents from antiquity to the present, it is hard to know where to begin and which events to include or exclude.

Other authors have penned comprehensive (if not entirely satisfactory) historical/political accounts of terrorism,[4] and I will not replicate their efforts here. Moreover, any verbal approach to understanding terrorism is woefully deficient: it cannot possibly depict the indescribable horrors of acts of violence that literally tear people apart. Nonetheless, despite the inherent limitations of this medium, this chapter of the book puts forward a brief "prehistory" of terrorism before focusing on what is probably considered the epicenter of contemporary terrorist activity—the Middle East. I conclude with some observations on past and prospective terrorist trends.

THE BLOODCURDLING DIALECTIC OF TERRORISM AND STATE TERROR

The Romans, Augustine argues, created a desert and called it peace. "Peace and war had a contest in cruelty, and peace won the prize."[5]

Jean Bethke Elshtain

Terrorizing ordinary men and women is first of all the work of domestic tyranny, as Aristotle wrote: "The first aim and end of tyrants is to break the spirit of their subjects."[6]

Michael Walzer

To designate a beginning point (or an end) of terrorism is arbitrary. When do (apparently) historical accounts of political acts involving actual and threatened violence commence? When do narrative accounts of murder begin? With the biblical tale of Cain and Abel? The *Tao De Ching*? Or perhaps with the *Mahabharata*?[7] Sometime during the ancient Egyptian, Chinese, Babylonian, Persian, or Roman Empires? Impossible to say. Nonetheless, other writers on this topic tend to begin their histories of terrorism about two millennia ago, and in the same part of the world that now seems so devastated by this phenomenon—what we now call "the Middle" or the "Near East."

From biblical times until the zenith of the Roman Empire (roughly from just before the time of Christ to the third century CE), the

Middle East comprised a hodgepodge of nomadic ethnic groups and city-states within what we now call the nation-states of Egypt, Israel (and Palestine), Tunisia, Libya, Greece, Jordan, Syria, Lebanon, Saudi Arabia, Iraq, the Gulf States, and Turkey. By the first century BCE, almost all these territories lay within the Roman Empire. It is here that the bloodcurdling dialectic between state terrorism (Terrorism from Above, TFA) and non-state terrorists (Terrorism from Below, TFB) may have begun, and—after some long intervals of relative peace, mainly under Islam—was revived during and shortly after World War I.

Many extant histories of warfare and terrorism begin their tragic tales with stories of "war heroes" and "epic struggles" in the ancient Near East, or the Mediterranean basin more generally. Some of these tales are entirely legendary—like the *Aeneid*. Others appear to have been largely based on actual events—like the "Histories" of Herodotos and Thucydides. And still others, like the *Iliad*, mix history and fiction. But these stories all depict the rise (and fall) of peoples and civilizations as rooted in wars and in related acts of individual and collective violence.

Warfare per se may have begun in the ancient Near East, specifically in what we today call Israel/Palestine. Archaeological remnants dating to the early Neolithic period (beginning about 8000 BCE)—most prominently the city of Jericho's walls and towers (about 7500 BCE)—suggest military fortifications, probably constructed against raiders and warriors from other tribes (aka "enemies").[8]

"Terrorism from Below" (TFB) itself is identified by numerous influential students of that subject with the political revolts and religious uprisings of Jewish opponents of Roman rule.[9] These accounts depict both the links between religion (or "religious fanaticism," aka "holy war/s" or "holy terror") and terrorism on the one hand, and, less clearly, between the TFB perpetrated by these "resistance fighters" and the widespread acts of political violence committed by the Romans (TFA) in their efforts to create, expand, and defend their empire against those who resisted Roman rule, most notably the German "barbarians" Jews, slaves, and early Christians.[10]

An Illustration of Terrorism: The Middle East

President George W. Bush, supported by some American Muslim clerics, once announced that Islam was "a religion of peace" that had been "hijacked" by al-Qaeda. But this apparently reassuring statement was immediately disputed by those who claimed instead that Islam is much more accurately seen as "the religion of war." In support they cited the Muslim belief that the world is divided by a continuous struggle between the *dar al Islam* (the unified house of Islam) and *dar al harb* (the house of the infidel); the Muslim believer is duty-bound to participate in this "holy war" (*jihad*).

It is true that belief in *jihad* is central to Islam, as is attested by many sacred texts (as is the necessity for "crusades" led by militant Christians). For example, as one *hadith* (saying of the Prophet Muhammad) proclaims: "There is no monasticism in Islam; the monasticism of this community is the holy war." It is also historically true that Islam began in battle. Exiled from his home for his subversive beliefs, the Prophet Muhammad gained warrior allies in the Saudi hinterlands, defeated his numerically superior opponents, and returned as a conqueror to his natal city of Mecca.

Muhammad was a great war leader as well as a spiritual redeemer, promising his followers not only admission to heaven in the next world, but also concrete spoils of victory in this one. Those early Muslims who did not participate in *jihad* were considered lacking in religious merit. Those who fell in battle were guaranteed immediate entrance into paradise.

Nor did Islam become a religion of peace after Muhammad's death (632 CE). Instead, Muslim warriors battled on against the vast and powerful Persian and Byzantine Empires; against all odds, they were victorious, validating for their millions of followers the authority of their message, as well as establishing the foundation for the great Islamic dynasties—Umayyad, Marwanid, Abbasid, Buyid, Fatimid, Seljuk, Ottoman, Safavid—which were eventually to rule from Morocco to Afghanistan. In other words, most Muslims never accepted the admonishment to render unto Caesar what is Caesar's. Instead, they sought to depose the party of Caesar (secular authority) and replace it with the party of God (divine authority).

Yet a portrait of Islam as a warlike religion is just as simplistic as the image of Islam as a religion of peace. Although many Muslims divide the world into warring camps of believers and unbelievers, in real life it is not so easy to decide who is who, since "only God knows" the true content of the human heart. As the great twelfth-century scholar and Sufi Muhammad al-Ghazali wrote: "Whoever says 'I am a believer,' is an infidel; and whoever says 'I am learned,' is ignorant"[11] Nor should a Muslim try to force others to recognize the truth, according to al-Ghazali. After all, the Quran itself says that God "leads astray whom He will and guides whom He will (16.95);" some will never believe, for "God has set a seal on their hearts" (2.6). The final word is that "the truth is from your Lord; so let whosoever will, believe, and let whosoever will, disbelieve" (18.28).

In this context, many Muslims have interpreted the injunction for *jihad* as a command to purify the self by ridding one's own heart of hypocrisy. With self-doubt, spiritual introspection, and resigned acceptance of the inevitable plurality of beliefs as major religious themes in Islam, war against the external heathen has usually been secondary to war against the internal Pharisee.

Nor has conversion to Islam by former non-believers usually been at the point of a sword; instead it has most often been a voluntary response to Muslim egalitarianism and the Prophet's expansive message of salvation. In this environment, Islamic pogroms against Jews, Christians, and other minorities were much less common in the premodern Middle East than in premodern Europe; all the descendants of Abraham (including Jews and Christians) were recognized as having a fundamental kinship with their Muslim brothers. For Muhammad did not repudiate the previous annunciations of Jesus or Moses. Rather, he saw his message as the restoration of earlier prophecies to their pure state. Thus, Muslim honor was generally satisfied with the payment of tribute from minority populations (the *dhimmi*), who in return were released from military service and other religious obligations.

The moral of this story is that it is easy to paint Islam as either essentially pacific or bellicose—just as it is easy to draw passages from the Bible or from the Torah to make either case about Christians and Jews. *The truth about all great religions is that the written record is ambiguous: Islamic scripture, like that of the Christians and Jews (or Hindus or Buddhists for that matter), can interpreted in various ways for various purposes.* In a real sense, it is the protean character of great religions that makes them so appealing, and so dangerous. . . . Islam is no different in this respect: its adherents can be pacifists or terrorists or somewhere in between; all can equally call on holy writ to "justify" themselves and their murderous deeds.

But an independent observer ought not be taken in by these claims; neither terrorism nor pacifism is reflective of some essential aspect of Islam, any more than the slavery and genocide that stain European history are a direct and inevitable consequence of the message of Jesus. With that caveat in mind, let us trace the history of terrorism and assassination in Middle Eastern Muslim societies, and explore its ideological and structural dimensions.

To begin, it is crucial to recognize that Islam is a *millennial* religion, a faith for which the millennial dream of the realization of the kingdom of heaven on earth was supposedly achieved, at least for a moment, during the rule of Muhammad and, for the Sunni tradition, the four rightly guided Caliphs (deputies) who succeeded him (Abu Bakr, Umar, Uthman, and Ali). To put it in Christian terms, it is as if, instead of being crucified, Jesus had become emperor and was then succeeded in that post by four of his close disciples. All of the majority (Sunni) Muslims look back on this era as a period in which human beings lived in a kind of earthly paradise, as a God-given justice prevailed among the believers. Ever since, virtually all Muslim rulers have been measured by this high spiritual standard, and have failed to live up to it. For some fundamentalist Islamic zealots, this failure has implied a state of permanent revolution: true believers must overthrow unjust rulers in the hope of bringing the redeemer (the *mahdi)* to power and thereby precipitating the "end of time."

Despite widespread Muslim nostalgia for the "golden days" of early Islam, this dynamic of disappointment and rebellion was at work at almost the very beginning of the Muslim polity, and was the source of schisms that continue to have repercussions even today. It began with the death of Muhammad. Immediately thereafter, the faithful had to live in a world where the Prophet no longer served as the living arbiter of good and evil, truth and falsehood.

Some of the Prophet Muhammad's tribal followers did not accept the rule of his elected successors, and considered them to be usurpers. Battles for power also ensued between the old pre-Islamic elite of Mecca, who were late converts, and those who had joined Muhammad earlier, but did not have such illustrious lineages. And resentment simmered about who had the right to control and distribute shares in the booty from conquest.

These antagonisms came to a head when the third Caliph Uthman favored his noble relatives with top administrative and military posts, inflaming the anger and jealousy of Muslims from rival lineages. In 656 CE, after a few days of heated disputes, these rivals killed Uthman. With Uthman's murder, the "door was opened" and *fitna* (chaos) was loosed in the world of Islam; that door would never again be closed.

Uthman's successor, the Prophet Muhammad's son-in-law Ali, struggled to gain control of the empire, but he was opposed by Uthman's allies, and especially by his cousin Muawiya, the military governor of Syria, who swore to revenge Uthman's death and to succeed him as caliph. Muawiya's success and Ali's death in 661 CE spelled the end of the "rightly guided Caliphate" and the beginning of secular rule that has dominated much of the Middle East ever since.

As Ignaz Goldziher puts it, henceforth the Sunni caliph became "nothing but the successor of the one who preceded him, having been designated as such by a human act (election, or nomination by his predecessor), and not entitled by the qualities inherent in his personality."[12]

However, many Muslims who had participated in Muhammad's community could not accept the disintegration of their unified and charismatic collective so easily. They nostalgically (and imaginatively) remembered the promises of the Prophet and the experience of the divinely consecrated commune of all Muslims (the *umma*)—memories (or longings) that continue today to activate religious resistance to secular government. Muslims have thus constantly sought more sanctified candidates to fill the post of ruler over an Islamic collective. *This quest, in its most extreme manifestations, has animated the unique brand of religious–political terrorism practiced in the name of Islam since the death of the Prophet Muhammad.*

For many Muslims, there have been two main approaches to reestablishing the sacred polity. The first was taken by those referred to as the *kharijites*, "those who go out." These originally were early tribal followers of Muhammad who later favored Ali against the alliance of military elites and Meccan aristocrats. But when Ali vainly sought negotiation with his enemies, the kharijites rejected him as a poseur and assassinated him. They then established radically egalitarian religious republics for themselves, wherein only the most pious and able would rule, regardless of family, ancestral spirituality, priority of conversion, or any other claim. In some kharijite groups, even women were given the same rights as men (something unknown or rejected by much of the rest of the Islamic world, and by non-Muslims as well, even today). Pitiless opponents of all who objected to their egalitarianism, the kharijites saw themselves as "the people of heaven" battling against "the people of hell." An ember of their moral fervor still burns in a sermon dating from 746 CE, execrating the Umayyads, who, the preacher says, "made the servants of God slaves, the property of God something to be taken by turns, and His religion a cause of corruption . . . . (they) said 'The land is our land, the property is our property, and the people are our slaves' . . . . The(se) people have acted as unbelievers, by God, in the most barefaced manner. So curse them, may God curse them!"[13]

W.M. Watt has portrayed the kharijites as a retrograde movement of disappointed tribesmen hoping "to reconstitute in new circumstances and on an Islamic basis the small groups they had been familiar with in the desert."[14] But unlike the pre-Islamic tribesmen, for the kharijites the rule of the strongest and cleverest was not enough; their leader also had to be the most devout. He could be deposed and even killed at any time, for any moral error, so that commanders rose and fell with rapidity.

Arguments over religious doctrines also continually split the kharijite bands. Although they were good at fighting, the loosely organized and internally divided kharijites could not gain any wider legitimacy or establish a stable governmental structure. They wasted themselves in unwinnable wars against much of the Muslim world, and against one another as well, in vain hopes of establishing an absolutely pure polity.

Despite an absence of political success, the kharijite impulse to high morality and political egalitarianism has had an affinity ever since with devout Muslim rebels who refuse to accept secular rule or elite domination. Even today, modern Islamist radicals—from the Muslim Brotherhood and Islamic Jihad in Egypt and the Saudi peninsula, to Jamaat-e-Islami in Pakistan, and to the Taliban and al-Qaeda in Afghanistan—are execrated by more orthodox clerics as "kharijites" because of their radical egalitarianism, moral self-righteousness, willingness to use violence against those with whom they disagree, and relentless opposition to central authority.[15] In turn, the Islamist radicals denounce their moderate opponents as apostates for accepting the "un-Islamic" commands of the corrupt and despotic rulers of secular Islamic state—whose political leaders are widely perceived to be manipulated and paid off by the West in general and by the United States in particular.

Although the rebellious and anarchistically inclined kharijites long were a thorn in the side of Middle Eastern authoritarian and repressive regimes, and though their message still has a powerful appeal, a more effective source of sustained sacred opposition to the status quo came from quite the opposite ideological direction. Instead of arguing for a radically egalitarian community of believers who freely elect as a leader the man best among them—as the kharijites had done—these rebels subordinated themselves to a sacred authority whose word was absolute law. For them, Muhammad's charisma was reincarnated in his descendants, notably in Ali, the Prophet's son-in-law and nephew, who served as the fourth caliph after the murder of Uthman. These are the Shi`ites, or "partisans" of Ali, who have argued that, since Muhammad had no sons, Ali had inherited Muhammad's spiritual power and must be recognized as Imam, the sacred ruler of all of Islam.[16]

For those following Ali or other lineal descendants of the Prophet, the problem of authority was solved by recognizing that one particular member of the Prophet's kin group had spiritual ascendance above all others, and therefore had the intrinsic right to rule. The Shi`ite belief in the omnipotence of their supposedly transcendental Imam has incited enthusiasm among the faithful, who could righteously unite behind him in a *jihad* against the perceived corruption of more centrist Muslims. But this also meant that their faith has often been severely challenged when the millenarian dream confronted political reality, and the faithful had either to accept disappointment of their hopes or embark on yet more fervent pursuits of the millennium.

The first crisis of faith occurred when Ali was assassinated by a poisoned sword wielded by a kharijite fanatic—an indication that assassination as a form of political terrorism began very early in the history of Islam. The kharijites had been early supporters of Ali, won over by his opposition to the entrenched interests of the Meccan elite. But they were furious when Ali compromised with his opponents after a stalemate in the Battle of Siffin in 658 CE. For kharijite zealots, any compromise was a bargain with Satan, and Ali had to pay for this betrayal with his life. Ali's son Husain was no more fortunate; he was abandoned by his allies and slaughtered with his followers by Muawiya's son Yazid at the Battle of Karbala in 680 CE—an event commemorated with weeping and expiatory self-laceration by Shi`ites ever since.

From Karbala until the present, Shi`ite resentment over Sunni rule and the perceived injustices of this world has fanned subversive acts of opposition, which have sometimes included terrorism. For example, the origins of the Abbasid dynasty (750–945 CE) lie in the actions of Shi`ite underground religious revolutionaries, the Hashimiyya, who aroused an alienated populace to revolt against the oppressive regime of the Marwanids. (This is another historical example of the dialectic between state terror and terrorist revolts against autocracies.) The Hashimiyya were experienced conspirators who recognized that an urban revolt in the center of the empire was impossible, but believed that a revolution from the margins could succeed. They identified Khurasan in Eastern Iran as the most likely place for such a revolt to begin.

A tiny, tightly knit group of extreme Islamic fundamentalists, the Hashimiyya used sophisticated techniques of recruitment and organization that closely resemble those of revolutionary Islamists today. Operating in small, segregated, highly disciplined, cells of true believers under strict central leadership, the Hashimiyya maintained absolute secrecy while spreading antigovernment propaganda and millenarian rhetoric. Overt rebellion started in the garrison town of Merv, where, in

747 CE, 2,200 rebels raised the black banner of revenge and revolution. They soon were joined by thousands of dissatisfied revolutionaries, and the movement swept Islamdom from east to west, ending in 750 CE with the ascent of the Abbasids and the beginning of a new imperial absolutism.

The leader of the Hashimiyya conspiracy in Khurasan was a shadowy figure, perhaps an ex-slave or bondsman, who is known to history only by his pseudonym, Abu Muslim Abdulrahman, born Muslim al-Khurasani ("a Muslim son of a Muslim, father of a Muslim of Khurasan"). This name was meant to indicate that he was neither client nor patron, neither Arab nor Persian, but was simply an ordinary Muslim from Khurasan. As M.A. Shaban says, "he was a living proof that in the new society every member would be regarded only as a Muslim regardless of racial origins or tribal connections."[17] Based on his promise of equality, Abu Muslim was able to unite a polyglot army of followers.

Not unexpectedly, one of the first acts of the Abbasid King whom Abu Muslim had placed on the throne was to organize Abu Muslim's assassination. The martyred hero has been popularly recalled ever since as a Messianic rebel who purportedly remains in hiding, awaiting the proper time to lead the people back to power. Abu Muslim was one of the first of such Muslim popular martyrs, who are called upon even today to justify popular rebellion against autocratic (usually secular) rulers. However, it is noteworthy that at Abu Muslim's death, there was no mass uprising. Very possibly most Muslims then, like most Muslims now, were satisfied to have a stable, if tyrannical, regime in power, following the local precept that "sixty years of an unjust Imam are better than one night without a Sultan."

Similar schismatic and redemptive millennial Shi`ite movements have periodically marked Muslim political history. For example, in the early tenth century CE, the Abbasids themselves were almost overthrown by the radically egalitarian Qarmatids, who mobilized supporters with the doctrine that the Messiah was soon to arrive and usher in the end of time. Retreating to the desert, these rebels forsook all traditional forms of socioeconomic distinctions and shared their property communally. They appealed to the latent idealism of the oppressed masses, attacked caravans of holy pilgrims, and in 930 CE committed the ultimate sacrilege by absconding with the Kaaba, the great stone in Mecca all Muslims face when they worship during the *hajj*. This powerful revolutionary movement only lost momentum when its military leader, Abu Tahir, named a young Persian as the actual Mahdi. Unfortunately for the Qarmatids, the new "Mahdi" soon distinguished himself by his insolence, ignorance, and cruelty. When he was executed, the movement lost its legitimacy and vanished. Other, more successful, Shi`ite movements include the Fatimids, who ruled Egypt from 969 to 1171, but collapsed as a result of internal dissension, and the Safavids, who conquered Persia in 1501 and became increasingly secularized and dissolute until their downfall in 1722.

But perhaps the most relevant historical precedent for the present is to be found in the extraordinary trajectory of a famous but quite small offshoot of the Fatimids: the Nizari branch of the Ismaili Shi`ites. The prototypical Assassins, they found refuge in several remote mountain enclaves at the very margins of the Seljuk Empire (in Turkey) at the end of the eleventh century.[18] Because of their fervor, their willingness to die for their beliefs, and their practice of assassination (always with daggers) as a political tool, the Nizari gave rise to legends of hashish-intoxicated madmen and mystical voluptuaries, dying at the whim of their mysterious master.[19] These legends disguised something even more remarkable: tightly disciplined communities of absolute believers, all imbued with a spirit that placed their ultimate mission above any personal desire—even above the desire for life. Although the Nizari Assassins did not intend to kill anyone but their political targets, they were the precursors of, and prototypes for, the self-sacrificing, suicidal bombers and terrorists who have spread from the Middle East (via a process akin to what Chalmers Johnson has called "blowback") throughout the entire world.[20]

The Nizari began under the charismatic leadership of the theologian and mystic Hasan al-Sabbah, the "old man of the mountain." Hasan argued that the spiritual authority of the Fatimid Imam was directly derived from a community of true believers whose absolute faith both defines and validates the Imam's mission. In order to manifest the reality of the Imam, the community of faithful Muslims must therefore devote itself completely and selflessly to bringing about his domination in the world. For this sacred purpose, *any means whatsoever could be employed*, including clandestine operations by undercover agents who remained hidden in place for years, awaiting the opportunity to kill their appointed targets. Their most famous victim was Nizam al-Mulk, the great Seljuk vizier, who was killed in 1092 in retaliation, so it was said, for the death of a Nizari carpenter—an indication of the millennial egalitarianism of the movement.

This case study prefigures the general historical tendency of religiously motivated terrorist groups to use terrorist tactics (such as assassinations) to achieve self-declared millenarian goals, and to rationalize murder by appealing to a "sacred" justification for their killing. It also exemplifies the "cycle of violence"—of murder "from above or below," and murderous retaliation by the victim's survivors against the perpetrators and anyone else unfortunate enough to be nearby when "payback" occurs. Terrorist acts of murder, and even more encompassing "counterterrorist" responses to these atrocities, persist to this day and are growing ever more global and lethal in scope.

Like most officially (U.S. government)–designated "terrorist" groups today, the Nizari were an isolated and relatively weak group who could not confront the might of the Seljuks and their allies directly. But the absence of any institutional means for passing down authority made assassination an effective tool for disrupting the empire. As Marshall Hodgeson puts it: "The shaykhs and amirs, a sage here and a ruler there, filling their offices by personal prestige rather than any hierarchical mechanism, were quite irreplaceable in their particular authority; when they were out of the way, the Isma`ilis could be free to establish their own more permanent form of power."[21]

Terrorism in the form of political assassinations was also used by the Nizari in tandem with positive reinforcement. Hodgeson tells the story of the anti-Ismaili theologian Fakhr ad-Din ar-Razi (died 1209) who was accosted by assassin, threatened with a dagger, and told that if he stopped his preaching, he would be given a regular bag of gold. When asked later why he ceased castigating the Nizari, Razi said "he had been persuaded by argument both pointed and weighty."[22] But despite their successes, the Nizari eventually abandoned assassination as a tactic and accommodated themselves to the Seljuk regime. The plain fact was that most Muslims then, as now, found assassination in particular, and political terrorism more generally, reprehensible, and would not follow Nizari leadership.

The trajectory of this archetypical band of religious terrorists is both unexpected and instructive. Most of the Nizari emigrated to India in the thirteenth century in order to escape the invading Mongol hordes. Now known as Khojas, they soon became wealthy entrepreneurs. Their present Imam, the Aga Khan, is reckoned to be the forty-ninth in the line. He is a thoroughly modern individual, but he is still the absolute spiritual leader of his flock—indicating that Shi`ite faith does not necessarily lead either to violence or to a repudiation of modernity. In fact, as many Christians have also discovered, there are distinct economic advantages in having one's divinely appointed spiritual guide right here on earth, especially under global capitalism (aka "modernization" and/or "globalization"). Al-Qaeda and other "successful" global terrorist organizations—and their Western adversaries—have long since discovered that even with "God on one's side," to conduct a "holy war" successfully, it does not hurt to have working modems and numbered Swiss bank accounts.[23]

We now come to the great oppositional Islamic upheaval of modern times, that is, the Iranian revolution of 1979, led by Ayatollah Khomeini. It is worth spending a few lines recapitulating the history of this movement since, along with the wholly secular regimes of Iraq (under Saddam Hussein) and North Korea, it is part of the "axis of evil" recently execrated by President Bush. Iran is also the most populous nation in the Middle East where Shi`ism predominates. Furthermore, throughout the Middle East as a whole, the Shi`ite clergy has had much greater independence than Sunni clerics, partly due to differences in the notion of spiritual authority (Sunni clerics are mainly interpreters of sacred text, while Shi`ites believe that certain scholars, known as Ayatollahs, are sacred authorities in themselves), and partly due to the Iranian clerisy's control over vast amounts of property. Because Iranian Ayatollahs have had such great spiritual authority and wealth, they have, until very recently, been able to resist secularizing trends in government, even prior to the advent of the Westernizing Reza Shah, who ought to sidestep Islam entirely by seeking legitimacy in a manufactured connection with pre-Islamic times, while looking to the secularized and Christian West as both his model for political development and military protector of his economic interests.[24]

The repressive policies of the Reza Shah and his successor led to great feelings of cultural alienation among the more traditional classes of Iran. Thus, the rise of Ayatollah Khomeini was not a great surprise, at least in retrospect. A brilliant scholar, a mystical teacher, a charismatic leader, he drew the materially disaffected and culturally dispossessed Iranian faithful to him, and as he did, his own unstated claim to be the manifestation of the redeemer appeared to them to be validated.

In his sermons, Khomeini repudiated the passive and submissive tendency within Shi`ism and appealed to its latent dreams of activism and transformation. True believers could now express their spirituality in terms of a cosmic revolution that would overturn all the stultifying dissimulation, guilt, and corruption of the past and reawaken the sacred community under Khomeini's ostensibly divine leadership—an eschatological event for which no amount of self-sacrifice was too great.

This change was symbolized when the coffins of young people killed fighting the Shah were paraded in the streets during the celebration of the martyrdom of Husain at Karbala. The message was that these new martyrs must not be abandoned as Husain had been. Meanwhile the shah was convincingly portrayed as the modern *Yazid*, a puppet of the (Western) "capitalist devils" and "The Great Satan" (aka the United States).

The old Shi`ite eschatology was reawakened, transformed, and reinvigorated by Khomeini and his acolytes; believers could now redeem the ancient stain of betrayal by actively purging this world of evil, starting in Iran and spreading to combat actively "The Great Satan," "the evil one." This message inspired impressive acts of self-sacrifice and ended in the overthrow of the shah, but also led to terrorist attacks against Americans and others.[25] *These violent assaults against both perceived political adversaries and civilian emissaries of despised foreign powers were justified on the grounds that in the battle against Satan, any methods were acceptable.* This is an age-old rationale for murder and terrorism, for the commission of acts of extreme violence purportedly "justified" by appeals to divine sanction. It is also a sanctification of the lethal tactics utilized by both those who would wage "holy war" against the West as well as by latter-day "crusaders" now conducting a "war against terror."

Khomeini's central claim was that he was refinding a divine order that had been lost. Said Arjomand calls Khomeini's message "revolutionary traditionalism."[26] Ironically, the "tradition" that was sought had actually never existed—though Khomeini and his followers argued that this was only because of a derailing of history due to purported Sunni treachery. From their perspective, the wrong turn of Islam occurred when Ali had been killed. To set right this historical injustice, Khomeini and his followers in Iran sought to take back the authority that had been denied them first by Sunni usurpers and then by the shah, and reunite the state and the faith. This sacred polity was to be ruled by an infallible Guide, a spiritual–political leader whose word "takes precedence over all other institutions, which may be regarded as secondary, even prayer, fasting and pilgrimage."[27]

The future of the Iranian revolution is still in doubt, and the matter is complicated by the structure of "dual power" in Iran, whereby the elected president and Parliament are ultimately beholden to an unselected "Council of Guardians" consisting mainly of antimodern Shi`ite clerics Loyal to Khomeini's message. Although democratizing and secularizing processes have been taking place since the 1990s, and the clergy has had to adapt itself to popular unrest or else risk an uprising, Iran remains a theocratic state.

Certainly the polarizing influence of Israel throughout the entire industrialized world[28] and most acutely within the Middle East is of central importance here, as Muslims of all political and religious stripes have become ever more willing to accept and even embrace terrorist martyrdom—with its "rewards" of scores of virgins in the afterlife and financial compensation for the "martyr's" family in this one—in the face of overwhelming Israeli military force.[29] For the Hezbollah (an Iranian-supported "terrorist" organization, according to the United States and Israel), this stance is supported by Shi`ite theology. But whether Iran can actually serve as a model for Sunni radicals is doubtful, since the whole basis of the Iranian revolution is not only anti-secularist and anti-Israeli, but also anti-Sunni, and is founded on a mythology of martyrdom that has no place is Sunni eschatology. This theological dispute, going back over a millennium, has made cooperation between militant Sunni Muslims (e.g., Iraq,) and Shi`ite "mujahidin" ("warriors of God," previously imported into Afghanistan by the United States and Saudis to fight the Soviets but now diffused throughout the entire region) extremely difficult if not impossible. The "connection," therefore, between al-Qaeda and Saddam Hussein's Baathists, if it exists at all, would be found in a *post*-U.S. invasion of Iraq, in order to forge a common front against the "infidel imperialists from the West."

A more appropriate model for Sunni revolutionary activism can be discovered in Sufism, which offers the Sunni equivalent to the charismatic personalism that is at the heart of Shi`ism. Sufism is concerned primarily with achieving a mystical communion with the deity, but it accomplishes this end within strictly hierarchical and often secretive holy orders (*tariqa*), which are focused around spiritual leaders (sheikhs or pirs) whose word is absolute law for the disciples. It therefore offers a prototypical organizational structure for the mobilization and inspiration of Islamic activists, *jihadists* ("holy warriors"). And in fact, during the first half of the twentieth century, many Sufi orders did serve as centers for resistance to British and French colonial authority.

Nonetheless, most present-day Muslim political activists have been quite hostile to popular Sufism. They maintain that Sufi practices are immoral innovations, and assert that the praise of Sufi saints and worship at saints' tombs are practices dangerously close to heresy. But despite their harsh ideological condemnation of Sufism, many fundamentalist Islamists have nonetheless gathered around charismatic figures and organized themselves in ways that closely resemble activist Sufi brotherhoods of the past.

For example, the radical Islamist Takfir wa al-hijrah ("excommunication and exile") group[30]—many of whom were imprisoned and executed after their assassination of the Egyptian minister of religious endowments—advocated a complete separation from secular society in preparation for their millenarian revolt against what they deemed to be the diabolical Egyptian state. Members of the sect (prefiguring al-Qaeda, which drew from its membership) were sworn to secrecy, bound together in tightly controlled and isolated units, rigorously instructed in techniques for self-purification, and enjoined to complete obedience to the leadership. All of them were under the command of an absolute leader, Shukri Mustafa, who claimed to know the secret meaning of every letter in the Quran, and whose word was regarded as sacred law.[31] Similar patterns are found in other radical Islamist sects, including al-Qaeda, and even the relatively moderate Muslim Brotherhood (in Egypt) developed secretive and inclusive cells (called families) that were held together by rigid discipline and a powerful faith in the spiritual supremacy of their leader, Hassan al-Banna, who himself came from a Sufi family and was given the Sufi title of *murshid* (Sufi equivalent of sheikh or emir).[32]

For most members of radical Islamist sects (which constitute the core of many "terrorist" groups in the Middle East and elsewhere), as for Sufis, once the true leader has been recognized, it is the duty of the disciples to emulate him and to offer him their absolute devotion. Their duty is to reject the corrupt society around them in order to replicate, within their own band of the spiritually elite, the original *umma* ("community of the Muslim faithful") gathered around the Prophet. A political party organized in this fashion then becomes the equivalent of the Sufi *tariqa*—a closed society serving as a training ground in purification of the soul. As in the *tariqa*, a hierarchy of dedicated disciples gains sacred knowledge through arduous study of texts written by the leader, public confession of sins, absolute obedience, and the practice of self-sacrifice. In the most extreme cases, this can mean terroristic martyrdom, usually but not always in the form of suicide bombings. Al-Qaeda is one example of this tendency.

However, terrorist actions by these cultic groups would have little popular resonance on "the Arab street" if it were not for one other aspect of terrorism in the Middle East—which is more pervasive and more influential than usually thought—*this is terror perpetrated by the state on its own people.*

In contrast to cultic terrorist organizations, state-sponsored terror very rarely makes any claim whatsoever to sacred justification. It is quite baldly the assertion of ruthless force for the express purpose of breaking and destroying any possible resistance or opposition to domestic tyranny and despotism. Such brutal violence is in part an indicator of the widely perceived illegitimacy of the secular state itself, which, from the earliest times, in the eyes of most Muslims has always suffered in comparison with the history of sacred rule by the Prophet and his caliphs.

Lacking any sacred credibility, popular compliance to the decrees of corrupt secular Muslim rulers (often perceived to be backed by the United States and other "infidel" nations) in the Middle East has generally been a direct result of the inculcation of mass terror from above, since otherwise a citizen would not willingly obey another man who is, in principle, no better than he is. Under these conditions, force can easily become its own argument. As one Muslim writes, the state then is popularly understood "as a source of evil and harm, and those who hold power tend to be unjust, to break the law, and to play with other people's lives. . . . Injustice is the rule, the abuse of power is the rule; the proper, adequate use of power is the exception."[33]

In former times, the violence and terrorism of Middle Eastern rulers were restrained both by traditional standards of honor and by the relative weakness of the regimes. As a consequence, most sultans (the word itself simply means "power") were content to torture, maim, and kill mainly members of their own immediate entourage, leaving the populace relatively unscathed as long as taxes were paid and peace maintained. However, contemporary Middle Eastern rulers (irrespective of their religious or political leanings) have much greater ambitions as well as greater means at their disposal for the infliction of violence and mass terror; as a result, state—sponsored terrorism in that region has greatly increased.

Iraq under Saddam Hussein may have been the most frightening and well-publicized instance of state terror, but the use of terrorism from above has been widely practiced throughout the entire region. A conservative estimate is that over 100,000 citizens "disappeared" during the reign of Saddam Hussein, and the number is probably closer to 250,000. Compare this to the 30,000 who "disappeared" during the "dirty war" in Argentina. Other regimes (from Algeria to Sudan, and from Libya to Taliban Afghanistan) have lesser, but equally horrifying, human rights records. We cannot understand the appearance of religiously based terrorist movements in the modern Middle East without also taking into account the way states there maintain their power through coercion of and violence against their own people.

Terrorism from above and from below reinforce each other in the Middle East as elsewhere across historical time and political space. The crucial difference between recent history and the past is that terrorism from below *has gone global*, and not been confined to the region, as evidenced by the attacks on the World Trade Center in 1993 and 2001. *But so has terrorism from above*, sometimes clad in the garb of "counterterrorism."

Political violence and terror(ism) have a long history in Middle Eastern Muslim societies. Whether they are more prevalent in this part of the world than elsewhere would require more extensive comparative work,[34] but it is clear that a deep sense of the illegitimacy of the secular state, coupled with a millennial tradition of charismatic leadership, can favor the rise of radical Islamist groups willing to use terror(ism) to bring the promised land into being. The popular appeal of such groups varies greatly, fluctuating according to the degree of oppression and alienation felt by the Muslim masses. Unhappily, at the moment, due to a combination of internal (corruption of indigenous leaders) and external (U.S. and Israeli policies) factors, it seems that both are on the rise.

TERROR AND STATE TERRORISM

"Terror," according to the dictionary definition, is a "*mode of governing*, or of opposing government, by intimidation." The "problem" for Western propaganda arises from the fact that the dictionary definition inconsiderately encompasses in the word "terrorist" Guatemala's Garcia or Chile's Pinochet, who clearly govern by the use of intimidation, but whose kindly ministrations in the interest of "stability" and "security" are best kept in the background. This calls for word adaptations that will exclude state terrorists and capture only the petty [?] terror of small dissident groups and individuals. All the establishment specialists and propagandists do in fact ignore Garcia, Pinochet, and the {white apartheid} South African government and concentrate on the lesser terror, by explicit or implied redefinition of "terrorist...." In short, we have been living not only in an age of age of escalating "terrorism" but in an age of Orwell, where words are managed and propaganda and scholarship are organized so that terror *means* the lesser terror—the greater terror [state terrorism] is defined out of existence and given little attention.[35]

Edward S. Herman

The danger of focusing exclusively on such *prima facie* acts of terrorism as the attacks on the World Trade Center in 1993 and 2001, and on suicide car bombings in the Middle East and Southeast Asia, is not just of minimizing or dismissing *the underlying reasons* for these atrocities, but of *missing "the forest for the trees," and of accordingly losing perspective*. All acts of TFB (the only kind of "terrorism" acknowledged by many Western intelligence agencies and political administrations) take place in specific historical, political, and religious–ideological contexts. This background is the omnipresent but frequently over-looked theater in which terrorist and counterterrorist bombings take center stage, that is, gain media headlines.

Moreover, as even Walter Laqueur (who is one of the strongest proponents of narrowing the definition of "terrorism" to TFB), notes, "Acts of terror carried out by police states and tyrannical governments ... have been responsible for a thousand times more victims and more misery than all actions of individual terrorism taken together."[36] While "body counts" are statistically and ethically questionable, the respective totals of victims killed during the twentieth century by nation-states and their surrogates (at least tens of millions, perhaps a hundred million or more), and by non-state terrorists (tens of thousands), leave no doubt as to who has been mostly responsible (Hitler's Germany, Stalin's Soviet Union, Mao's China, Hirohito's Japan, Pol Pot's Cambodia, France and United Kingdom before and after World War II, the United States during much of the latter half of the twentieth century, as well as the governments of many African, Latin American, and Southeast Asian "client" states of the West) for the commission of mass murder on a global scale.[37]

According to Johan Galtung and William Blum, the United States has been the most "rogue" of "rogue-states," having conducted almost 70 "interventions" in other countries since 1945, almost half of which have involved bombings (and, hence, civilian casualties).[38] This is on top of what Galtung calls the "structural violence"—of poverty, mass hunger and disease, and exploitation—that afflicts billions of people in countries whose natural and human resources are appropriated by the United States, its allies, and local minions, for their own purposes.

Virtually all governments "justify" their terrifying acts of violence against "enemies" and the "states" (mainly civilian populations) that harbor them by lofty appeals to "national security," the "right to self-defense," and, ironically, "for the sake of peace." But so do their adversaries, both terrorists from above and from below. ... Their victims are almost universally either dehumanized ("collateral damage") or left without appeal.

From the points of view of the *perpetrators of individual* acts of "terrorism," their deeds are justified responses to the "evil" and murderous activities of *nation-states*, today most prominently Israel and the United States.[39] In other words, from the perspective of officially designated "terrorists," not only is their cause just, but the violent means they employ to serve that cause (often "jihad") is also a *legitimate response* to the *greater* violence perpetrated against their peoples and families by military, economic, cultural, and ideological "imperialists and oppressors."

The "greater terror and violence" committed by nation-states against their own and "enemy" civilians is, from this point of view, appropriately answered by what the philosopher Ted Honderich denotes "liberation terrorism, terrorism to get freedom and power for a people when it is clear that nothing else will get if for them." According to Honderich, the "outstanding case" of "liberation terrorism" is the struggle of Palestinians, who "have exercised a moral right ... (in their terrorism against the state-terrorism and war of the Israelis) as certain as was the moral right ... of the African people of South Africa against their white captors and the apartheid state."[40] The problem, of course, is that *every* side claims to have the "moral right," to have God and history on their side, and to do violence and wage war "for the sake of peace .... "

For example, like their Western adversaries, many present-day Islamic *jihadists* and other "terrorists" believe that they "are not in favor of violence for its own sake .... (but) are for peace. We believe in the teachings of the Prophet—we will not attack anyone unless we have to." They also tend to believe that their acts of violence against "God's enemies" (Israel and the West) will be rewarded in the next world: "Life after death is forever.... So it's very important that you lived your life for Allah, so you are rewarded after death. God looks at those who sacrifice their lives in the jihad with love. God is with me."[41] A Palestinian suicide bomber, a member of the Al Aksa Martyrs Brigade who killed himself and at least eight other passengers aboard a bus in Jerusalem, said, according to a report in *The New York Times*, the attack was retaliation against the "Nazi wall" constructed by Israel, as well as revenge for an Israeli military raid into the Gaza Strip that killed 15 Palestinians.[42]

The logic of such a position, however, is what Martin Luther King, paraphrasing the Bible, called "an eye for an eye, and a tooth for a tooth," which, if followed to its conclusion, leaves everyone on Earth blind and toothless. This may well be the ultimate termination of an "unending war against terror and terrorism." For if every surviving friend or relative of every casualty of this "war" were to avenge the loss of their loved one(s),[43] and/or every state were to respond militarily against the perpetrators of a terrorist attack on its soil, the outcome would be never-ending series of attacks and counterattacks, leading to possible annihilation.

All sides in this mortal conflict bear the responsibility for the terrorization of the vast majority of the human race who do not wish to take part in, or to support, what the physicist Herbert York (in describing the nuclear arms race) has called the "race to oblivion." But it is the powerful nation-states of the world that are ultimately responsible for historically initiating a "reign of terror" (originally a *positive* self-description of early French revolutionists, the Jacobins)[44] against domestic political opponents and for expanding a "war against terrorism" to encompass the entire planet.

"JUST" AND "UNJUST" WAR(S) ON TERROR AND TERRORISM?

How is justice served by the use of force? For Augustine, a resort to force may be an obligation of loving one's neighbor, a central feature of Christian ethics.... The historic just war tradition grappled with Augustine's statement that war may be resorted to in order to preserve or to achieve peace—and not just any peace, but a just peace that leaves the world better off than it was prior to the resort to force.... As the theologian Joseph E. Capizzi writes: "According to Augustine, nonviolence is required at the individual level and just war mandated at the societal level...." Particularly useful is the tough-minded moral and political realism of just war thinking—not a Machiavellian "anything goes" realism, but an Augustinian realism that resists sentimentalism and insists on ethical restraint. Estrangement, conflict, and tragedy are constant features of the human condition, and just war thinking laced with Augustinian realism offers no assurances that we can ever make the world entirely safe.[45]

Jean Bethke Elshtain

These conditions (...if and when they are free and voluntary, performed at the subject's... express wish or desire ...) are of necessity absent in the case of the deliberate (and unintended but foreseeable) killing of innocents in war, terrorism, and other kinds of violence, and so leave the universal principle of innocent immunity intact in relation to them.[46]

Haig Khatchadourian

Emmerich de Vattel...in 1758 ... (in) his enormously influential study *The Law of Nations*...advanced the shocking idea that is pointless to talk about which cause in a given war is just; every party believes its own to be and can almost never be shaken from that conviction. The true indicator of which side carries the right, Vattel continued, is not the relative merit of antebellum claims but something much easier to assess and judge: the behavior of belligerents during actual hostilities.[47]

Caleb Carr

Efforts to provide ethical justifications for the initiation and conduct of war date back to the Code of Hammurabi (during the eighteenth century BCE in ancient Babylon, located in what is now called Iraq) and were developed further by the Greeks and Romans in numerous treatises and legislative codes.[48] In his *History of the Peloponnesian War*, for example, the great Greek historian Thucydides (re)constructs a heart-rending dialogue between the morally appealing magistrates of the small city-state of Melos (a Spartan colony without the means to defend itself) and the politically tough-minded ("realpolitik") generals of Athens, who attacked this island in 416 BCE, ostensibly because of Melos's association with Athens' mortal rival, the city-state of Sparta.

Thucydides fashions his dialogue to highlight the glaring cap between the Melian appeals to "justice and fairness" and what the ancient Greek critic Dionysius calls the "depraved shrewdness" of the Athenian conquerors. The Melians, who had never done the Athenians any harm, tried—*in vain*—to appeal to their sense of "fair play." According to Thucydides, the Athenians told the Melians: " . . . you have never done us any harm . . . the standard of justice depends on the equality of power to compete and that in fact the strong do what they have the power to do and the weak accept what they have to accept. . . . It is a general and necessary law of nature to rule wherever one can. This is not a law we made ourselves, nor were we the first to act upon it when it was made. We found it already in existence, and we shall leave it to exist for ever among those who come after us. We are merely acting in accordance with it, and we know that you or anybody else with the same power as ours would be acting in precisely the same way."[49]

From the standpoint of virtually all ethical traditions, the Melians had "right" on their side, but the Athenians had something vastly more powerful in this world—might. Consequently, the Melians did not attempt to resist, relying, unwisely, on the Athenians' presumed compassion and mercy. The Athenians slaughtered all Melian males of military age, enslaved their women and children, and colonized Melos.

In the Peloponnesian War, as in virtually all wars to follow, high-minded appeals to justice fell on deaf ears. The Athenian "cause" (to defeat Sparta) was irrelevant to those who fell victim to the quasi-genocidal means adopted by the generals to advance it. Hence, the Augustinian distinction (advanced in the fourth century CE to justify Christian participation in the defense of Rome against its "barbarian" enemies) between *Jus ad Bellum* (Latin for the "justice of going to war") and *Jus in Bello* ("justice in a war") usually becomes merely "academic" once hostilities have begun.

The doctrine of "just and unjust wars" was originally formulated by Augustine—and refined by theologians from Aquinas to the present and by Catholic councils from the Second Lateran Council in 1215 to the Second Vatican Council in 1966—to place *restraints on* the conduct of combatants during war. These restraints are summarized in two principles, *double effect* (or *proportionality*), and *discrimination* (or *noncombatant immunity*).[50] The principle of proportionality asserts that for a war to be "just," its overall moral benefits must it exceed its overall moral costs; the principle of discrimination recognizes that while civilians ("noncombatants") will usually be killed during wars, they *must not be direct, intentional* objects of military hostilities. However, this principle further assumes that civilian noncombatants are, in fact, often the "indirect" targets of such activities, and as long as civilians have been "unintentionally" targeted, those who do the targeting are not morally culpable for the "unintentional" effects (civilian injuries and deaths) of such wartime "necessities" as sieges and bombings.

In practice, however, such fine-sounding discriminations are usually lost. Siege, for example, perhaps the oldest tactic of "total war,"[51] has been routinely employed by invading armies against the civilian populations of "enemy" cities, from antiquity to the recent past (as in the Nazis' siege of Leningrad from 1941 to early 1944, during which time more than a million Russian civilians succumbed to disease and famine).[52] In 72 CE, the Romans laid siege to Jerusalem, which, according to the Roman historian Josephus, had been seized by the "fanatical Zealots" (Western history's first "terrorists"). The deaths—by starvation, illness, and wounds—of many Jewish noncombatant residents of Jerusalem, were certainly foreseeable and predictable. Whether the Romans explicitly "intended" to cause the death of a specific Jewish citizen of Jerusalem is beside the point. The Romans were culpable for the suffering and deaths of those whose cities they besieged, just as their "fanatical" Zealot "terrorist" opponents were responsible for the murders of numerous Romans they assassinated.

Both state terrorists wearing imperial uniforms, *and "freedom fighters"* who claim they are opposing imperialism and tyranny, *commit murder,* ostensibly to further their political causes. The result is that the "wars" they conduct are *neither "just" nor "unjust,"* for they *are beyond any moral or legal appeals* to justice (either as "fairness" or as "retribution") that can be made by the victims of their Killers' murderous methods. To demonstrate the "justice" or "injustice" of a particular action, the victims of such acts need to be able to be heard in a public forum, one in which those who are tried for injustices such as "war crimes" (against civilians) may be held accountable and punished. But until the end of the twentieth century—when an International Court of Justice was established in The Hague along with *ad hoc* war crimes tribunals to try selected political and military leaders for "crimes against humanity," and Commissions of Truth and Reconciliation were set up in South Africa and elsewhere to bring together war criminals and their surviving victims—the victims of war crimes have rarely if ever had the chance to confront their torturers, unless, of course, they happened to be on the winning side.

The "justice" or "injustice" of a particular war (from the Peloponnesian War, which was "won" by the Spartans to today's "global war on terror," which may or may not have a clear "victor") has almost always historically been determined by the military victors. For example, some Germans and Japanese generals and politicians who, during World War II, ordered and/or conducted "genocidal" operations, including "terror bombings," against their enemies, were found legally culpable for their actions and were punished as "war criminals." But British and American generals and politicians who ordered and/or conducted terror bombings of civilian populations during the same war have been lionized as "war heroes," because they defeated the axis powers.[53]

Former Yugoslav President Slobodan Milosevic, who is being tried as a "war criminal" in The Hague, decries the "double standard" being employed by his accusers (jurists and political leaders from the NATO countries that bombed Serbia and Kosovo in 1999), who are not themselves on trial for having killed many civilian noncombatants during those bombings. While Milosevic may personally be culpable for crimes against humanity, his logical point is valid: unless "victors" of wars are judged by the *same* standards as the vanquished, there persists a legal and moral double standard according to which a particular war is "just" if the victors deem it so, and particular acts of violence committed during a war are "just" or "unjust" (and hence "criminal") if the jurists on the winning side so decree.

The consequences of such wartime activities as sieges and bombings of cities are *perfectly foreseeable and predictable*: many people who have no part in a war, except for having the misfortune to be in the wrong place at the wrong time, will suffer and die; and most people who carried out the operations resulting in these injustices will not be held accountable (except possibly by their consciences). *This is the real logic and morality of war*, and it is one that undermines the very "legitimacy" of intellectual efforts to discriminate between "just" and "unjust" wars. From the points of view of most wartime victims, wars are neither "just" nor "unjust." They are mass murders. And those decision-makers and warriors who initiate and conduct mass murders committed during wars should be held accountable to the same legal and moral standards as criminals who murder during peacetime.

The millennia-long effort to distinguish between "just" and "unjust" wars is a "category mistake." For it is based on two false premises: the first is the mistaken assumption that universally agreed-upon ethical and legal standards of "justice" and "injustice" are uniformly applicable to "war" in general and to particular wars, as well as to "unjust" acts committed during wars. Justice and injustice, equity and inequity, fairness and its opposite, are ethical and legal categories that are notoriously elusive and, furthermore, to a significant degree are also culturally variable. To presume the existence of one uniform, worldwide, historically invariant standard of justice upon which rational people might agree is dubious. Further to assume that a universal notion of justice, were one to be consensually validated, might be *uniformly applied, especially during "the fog of war" and its aftermath,* beggars the imagination. *And legal/ethical notions such as justice would, like everything and everyone else, disintegrate entirely during and after a "war" involving the significant usage of weapons of mass destruction.*

The second incorrect assumption underlying the notion of "just and unjust" war—namely, that there is "*war*" to which notions like "justice" and "injustice" may be applied—is refuted by the fact that no two wars are alike, and neither are any two "crimes" committed during a war. There is no "war" per se—there are only wars. Moreover, even if there were to be a consensus as to which wars were "just" or "unjust," and which wartime activities were "criminal"—which there is not—the mechanisms now available impartially to capture, try, and punish "war criminals" (assuming there were global agreements as to who the candidates were for this dubious title) are woefully inadequate. But they are all we have.

The International Criminal Court is a step in the right direction, as are resolutions passed by the UN Security Council and General Assembly. But the opinions of this World Court are merely advisory, and many nations (including but not limited to such "rogue-states" as Iraq, North Korea, Israel, and the United States) routinely flaunt them. Security Council Resolutions of the United Nations are frequently violated, or evaded, and mandates of the General Assembly often fall on deaf ears (namely, the leaders of nation-states not in agreement with them). Hence the punishment for violating internationally agreed-upon legal codes and moral norms (which are the least imperfect operationalizations of "justice" now available) may vary widely or may be nonexistent.

THE TERRORS OF HISTORY AND THE STATE OF TERROR

> History is terror because we have to move into it not by any straight line that is always easy to trace, but by taking our bearings at every moment in a general situation which is changing.[54]
>
> Maurice Merleau-Ponty

> The chief reason warfare is still with us is neither a secret death wish of the human species, nor an irrepressible instinct of aggression, nor, finally and more plausibly, the serious economic and social dangers in disarmament, but the simple fact that no substitute for this final arbiter in international affairs has yet appeared on the political scene....Nor is a substitute likely to appear so long as national independence, namely, freedom from foreign rule, and the sovereignty of the state, namely, the claim to unchecked and unlimited power in foreign affairs, are identical.[55]
>
> Hannah Arendt

The division of the world into "sovereign" nation-states, each with its own sense of "national security" and few with adequate allegiance to the global imperative of "common security," is, as Arendt and others have pointed out, a, perhaps *the*, chief reason for the alarming increase in the number and lethality of wars and other forms of violent conflict during the past century.[56] Beginning with the French Revolution and its aftermath, continuing through World Wars I and II and the precarious "balance of nuclear terror" during the period of the Cold War (1945-91) between the United States and the Soviet Union, and culminating, perhaps, with the "global war on terror/ism," nations and their leaders—especially those with imperial ambitions—have increasingly put at peril not only their own security but the very existence of life on Earth.[57]

The increase in the number and lethality of wars has historically proceeded in tandem with the rise and dispersion of what are somewhat euphemistically called "weapons of mass destruction" (aka WMD, including but not limited to nuclear, chemical, and biological weapons), which, if deployed in significant numbers, could induce a "cold and dark nuclear winter" upon this planet, and effectively end civilization, if not life on Earth.[58] This would truly be the end of history. And it would likely be precipitated because those states and groups in possession of such weapons, feeling "insecure" and perhaps "terrified" by the danger of "losing," decided to use them rather than lose them. They might no longer be "deterred" by the prospect of annihilation (the "logic of deterrence," of "MAD"—Mutually Assured Destruction—which allegedly restrained the behavior of the United States and the Soviet Union during the Cold War)[59] but might instead choose to sacrifice themselves, their nations, and perhaps humanity, rather than be "defeated." Such is the psycho-logic of what Robert J. Lifton and Richard Falk have called "nuclearism,"[60] or the "superpower syndrome" but, which is regrettably no longer confined to two nuclear "superpowers." Like the weapons themselves, the psycho-logic (perhaps more accurately, psychosis) of nuclearism (no longer confined to *nuclear* weapons) is proliferating.

In tandem with nuclearism coexists the double standard regarding WMD possession and proliferation—which is tolerated if done by nations (such as Israel, Pakistan, and India) perceived to be friendly to the West, and decried if attempted by candidates for membership in the "Axis of Evil" (including Iraq, Iran, and North Korea). Non-proliferation treaties and enforcement provisions, not to mention virtually all ethical and logical norms, stipulate that all nations seeking weapons of mass destruction should be persuaded (such as Libya) or compelled not to acquire them, and that all nations possessing them should demonstrate evidence of reducing, and eventually eliminating, WMDS. The lamentable fact that *just the opposite is occurring* (despite some modest reductions in American and Soviet *strategic* nuclear forces) indicates the unflagging determination of both nuclear and nuclear-wannabe states to "modernize" their existing nuclear arsenals and to continue to acquire the means (ranging from intercontinental ballistic missiles to suitcases) to deliver them. In an age of "loose nukes" and "preemptive wars," despite public (mis)perceptions to the contrary, the danger of "intentional" or "accidental" nuclear war remains high.[61] The state of nuclear terror is global, even if most people elect not to acknowledge it.

The historical dialectic of terrorism from above and from below, of rulers and tyrants who terrorize their peoples and of insurgents who employ the terror-inducing means to oppose them, probably arose, like history itself, several millennia ago in the ancient Near East. The termination of this, and our, history may likewise commence in that same part of the world, unless the psycho-logic, or psychosis, that generates state terror and terrorism is overcome, and none too soon.

If war became terrorism during the twentieth century, terrorism has become global war during this century. It is an asymmetric war between the unmatched military power of the industrialized world, led, willingly or unwillingly, by the United Sates, and a decentered, shifting congeries of groups and individuals, not all of them Muslim, who oppose, by any means necessary and with the sacrifice of their own lives, what they perceive to be the global hegemony of an "infidel" imperial state.[62] And the hatred and resentment felt by many people in the Middle East and elsewhere, is spreading, since violent responses by the United States and Israel against terrorists—as well as against the states in which they live and the civilian populations who are unfortunate enough to be caught in the middle—not only kill many innocent people, but enrage their survivors, destabilize "moderate" governments, and facilitate the recruitment of young men and women to fight the "Great Satan" and its allies, especially Israel.[63] As former U.S. president Jimmy Carter has said, "We sent Marines into Lebanon and you only have to go to Lebanon, to Syria or to Jordan to witness first-hand the intense hatred among many people for the United States because we bombed and shelled and unmercifully killed totally innocent villagers—women and children and farmers and housewives—in those villages around Beirut. . . . As a result of that . . . we became kind of Satan in the minds of those who are deeply resentful. This is what precipitated the taking of our hostages and that is what has precipitated some of the terrorist attacks—which were totally unjustified and criminal."[64]

Furthermore, as the French theorist Jean Baudrillard claims, we are witnessing the *escalation* of this conflict of "terror against terror . . . (in which) the repression of terrorism spirals as unpredictably as the terrorist act itself. No one knows where it will stop . . . ."[65]

But the *greatest* terror, today as in the ancient world, is being perpetrated by imperial states, particularly the nuclear states, against those who would oppose their rule over Earth. The violent responses of contemporary terrorists to that dominion are morally reprehensible but politically understandable. In the short run, they will *not* succeed in defeating the United States and its allies, any more than other terrorist groups—from the Zealots to the Russian anarchists of the late nineteenth and early twentieth centuries—by using "targeted assassinations," succeeded in overthrowing the Roman and Romanoff Empires. *Those* empires did *eventually* implode, due to a combination of internal and external pressures. And the American imperial state will, like all its predecessors, do so as well—most likely not because of the murderous acts of terrorists but rather as a consequence of "imperial overreach."

To "end" terror and terrorism will be an exceedingly difficult, if not impossible, challenge to all of humanity during the beginning of this new millennium. There are a few historical precedents, not all of them encouraging, for confronting, and surviving, terror and terrorism. They may provide us with some measure of hope, if not with complete reassurance. It is to the historical memories and experiences of the survivors of political terror that I now turn.

3

ARTICULATING THE INEFFABLE
THE VOICES OF THE TERRIFIED

This is not an Orthodox Jewish thought, but the bad are rewarded and the good are punished . . . this is the way how things are going. . . . I'm a very good person and sometimes have seen bad people get rewarded. . . . If you say you're a Holocaust survivor, people become guilty . . . the border between normality and abnormality in life and war is very thin. . . . The fact that people are bad and want to murder one another is more normal than we like to think . . . ! I feel very terrorized, so fear is a normal feeling for me. . . . Everyone in the world can be dangerous. . . . That is what I learned in the war, even if I didn't see people die. . . . The Germans were allowed to become sadists, based on my camp experience. . . . You are like them . . . It can happen that normal, civilized people can also become murderers. . . . If you remember that, then maybe it won't happen as often. . . . It can happen everywhere![1]

Dutch male Holocaust survivor

Psychological trauma is an affliction of the powerless. At the moment of trauma, the victim is rendered helpless by overwhelming force. When the force is that of nature, we speak of disasters. When the force is that of other human beings, we speak of atrocities. . . . The ordinary response to atrocities is to banish them from consciousness. Certain violations of the social compact are too terrible to utter aloud: this is the meaning of the word *unspeakable*.[2]

Judith Herman

BOMBED . . . FROM BELOW . . .

It began like any other day, but it would be a day like no other. In a moment, this "very Catholic," 46-year-old Spanish nurse's life would change forever, and not for the better.

It was a clear late October day in Madrid. "SPB" was walking down the street preoccupied with her thoughts and daily tasks when a car passed by her and stopped.[3] "There was an explosion and I was thrown in the air, landed next to a wall close to a garden, hit the curb. It was horrible! I woke up and wasn't aware of anything, forgot everything.... My purse was on fire, leg and pants were cut. I saw a bus full of smoke inside ... was in shock, was shaking, terrified, very scared, looked around and everything was dark.... In front of me was a burned-out car and ... dead people ... was very scared."[4]

Police came, took her to an ambulance. The left side of her head hurt, she was bleeding, and her left boot was on fire. There was a sound/noise inside her ear; shrapnel injured her.... "Was terrible! It was a car bomb." (SPB then starts sighing and cries intermittently during the rest of the interview.) "I knew that God was leaving me on earth, and I didn't stop praying the whole time" (during surgery in the hospital). "My ears and eyes still hurt, sounds all the time in my ears, have vertigo, had therapy for psychological problems. I feel empty and want to know more about what happened."[5]

It was not until three months after the attack that SPB was told that six people had died and sixty others were injured during this attack. ETA was responsible, she sighs: "They use car bombs to try to get separate from Spain.... Spanish people who believe in God hope ETA can disappear."[6]

SPB reports having memory problems. Unlike many other survivors of terrorist attacks, she was fortunate to have had strong family support: her sister and two children took care of her during her two–four months of recuperation. But she still has nightmares (she sighs, cries), as well as "a lot of panic, fear, and anxiety." To address these problems, SPB sees a psychiatrist, takes sleeping and antianxiety pills, has started smoking again, and has flashbacks.

Like her mother, this self-reported "very Catholic" lady believes in God and in an afterlife: "God forgives everything, but the punishment is here on earth. Good people have a special place in heaven." But the bombers escaped.

SPB felt terrified then (the attack occurred on October 30, 2000) and still feels terrified, more than three years later. She is always afraid, but is not particularly vindictive: "Terrorists behave without reason. Talk with them and put them in prison." She adds how she feels almost always in pain, but has no solidarity with Spanish government officials, "whose first goal should be to take care of the victims of terrorism" (and don't).

An apolitical daughter of Socialist partisans of the Republic during the Spanish Civil War, SPB gave me a book she herself has written about her experiences, thanked me and the interpreter, slipped out of the Madrid café where we met for coffee, and scurried away into the pale sunlight of a late-autumn Spanish midday.

Clinically speaking, SPB is the quintessential bearer of a psychological malady called "Posttraumatic Stress Disorder" (PTSD). According to the "bible" of (North) American psychiatry and psychotherapy, the *Diagnostic and Statistical Manual of Mental Disorders* (*Fourth Edition*), "the essential feature of Posttraumatic Stress Disorder is the development of characteristic symptoms following exposure to an extreme traumatic stressor involving personal experience of an event that involves actual or threatened death or serious injury.... *The person's response to the event must involve intense fear, helplessness, or horror....* The characteristic symptoms resulting from the exposure to the extreme trauma include persistent experiencing of the traumatic event, persistent avoidance of stimuli associated with the trauma and numbing of general responsiveness, and persistent symptoms of increased arousal....The full symptom picture must be present for more than 1 month, and the disturbance must cause clinically significant distress or impairment in social, occupational, or other important areas of functioning. Traumatic events that are experienced directly include, but are not limited to, military combat, violent personal assault...being kidnapped, being taken hostage, *terrorist attack, torture, incarceration as a prisoner of war or in a concentration camp*, natural or manmade disasters, severe automobile accidents, or being diagnosed with a life-threatening illness."[7]

Despite her strong religious convictions, apparently sturdy physical constitution, and many social and familial supports, this middle-aged Spanish survivor of a classic terrorist attack "from below" is acutely anxious and is plagued by virtually all the symptoms listed under PTSD. In chapter 4, the topography of this jarring "internal world" is explored in more detail. But here, the terrain of the "external world" of the faces, bodies, and limbs of survivors of terrifying political attacks is described in more phenomenological detail.[8]

Cut back to Madrid in early December 2003. A 30-year-old Spanish male, originally from Andalucia, is running a center for the victims of terrorism. With good reason.... Three years earlier, "SPA's" father, then attorney general of a Spanish province, was assassinated by ETA.

On October 9, 2000, SPA was relaxing near a swimming pool in his home town of Malaga. He got a phone call from his aunt/uncle saying his father has "suffered a terrorist attack and was in extremely bad condition." SPA says: "I almost fell into the pool but didn't cry" (when he heard from his aunt that his father had died after having been shot in the mouth by two guys). He later heard on the radio that his father was "clinically dead," and he then went to the hospital in Granada, where the attack had occurred. ETA called the police to claim responsibility since SPA's father was, in ETA's view, "a judicial symbol of the oppressive Spanish state." SPA's mother "remained strong but was devastated." He "later felt guilty about not crying, but suffered deep inside without expressing it because he didn't want the terrorists to get that satisfaction."[9] He cried years later.

SPA says all members of his family (his mother, one younger brother, and two younger sisters) had the same dreams/nightmares about their father being killed by ETA. He claims he also had premonitions, precognitive dreams about the assassination, and that it was déjà vu when it "came true." But SPA reports that the dreams stopped the same day as the assassination. He has had "one or two nightmares" about terrorist attacks since then, and has still has dreams about fighting terrorism, but says "I'm not obsessed with it but am determined to fight terrorism."[10] The most conspicuous symbol of the peril of even an exclusively nonviolent "fight" against terrorism is the fact SPA's office in central Madrid is unlisted.

SPA blames both ETA and the Spanish government (for not protecting his father with bodyguards, since other officials had also been murdered in Andalucia) for the death of his father. The assassins were caught, confessed, and sentenced to prison terms of 30 years (the maximum in Spain). He believes a nonviolent alternative (to terrorist assassinations and car bombings) would be for ETA to be in "dialogue" with Spanish government officials, possibly to change the Spanish constitution to permit independence for the Basque country (for which, in SPA's view, there is "no legal or political basis"). But "ETA can't achieve its goal." (He then showed me a document he wrote about ETA's history.) "*Terrorism in general just doesn't make any sense. It uses violent means to achieve political and religious goals they think are worthwhile.... It's a different way of waging war.*"[11]

Like his parents, SPA is a practicing Roman Catholic and an "eclectic" Christian Democrat (who now "votes for the person, not the party"). Both his parents were Christian Democrats, and his mother a professor of political science and sociology.

SPA believes in an afterlife and in God: "Everybody pays for what he's done in this life, but a terrorist doesn't have to go to hell if he changes his life and is redeemed.... I believe in peace...I feel threatened but not terrified."[12] He concludes the interview by stressing the importance of human rights, and he criticizes both ETA and the Basque regional government for what's happened in Spain.

SPA seems very reflective, precise, and sensitive. He *seems to have been terrified, but not traumatized,* by the tragic death of his father. . . .

The next day, I interviewed another Spanish female, "SPC," who was 20 years old when *her* father was assassinated by the *Commandos Autonomos Anticapitalistas* (*CAA*), in San Sebastian, on March 26, 1982. At that time, SPC's father had been director of the local telecommunications company in the Basque region; her mother was a housewife. Both parents were nonpracticing Catholics, and they had "not much politics." SPC is agnostic, a lawyer, and Socialist. She also gave me a book she wrote about her experiences with terrorism.

On the day of her father's assassination, SPC was in Bilbao (also in the Basque region). Because her father had been threatened in the past, there were body guards at home. They did not help. . . .

According to the police who broke the terrible news to her, three masked gunmen shot and killed her father and a body guard. She was told by a policeman in the hospital where her father died that it "was clear it was a terrorist attack." SPC had long been afraid her father would be killed because he "represented the interests of the Spanish state telecommunications company." (Her tone was very emphatic and demonstrative, involving the use of much body language—possible somatization in psychotherapeutic terms—but no crying.) The terrorist group (*CAA*) sent a message to the media claiming responsibility for the attack.

At the hospital, SPC didn't believe her father was dead until she saw his body. Then she started crying, yelling, and screaming. She was very agitated, perhaps manic. . . .

SPC says she blocked out what happened next (with the police), who were "cold, insensitive and didn't know how to treat people in my condition. . . . There was no psychological counseling then. . . . It began only in the 1990s."[13]

Although SPC says she didn't feel personally threatened at that time, after some years, she decided to have bodyguards whenever she went to the Basque country. And now she reports being threatened because she "is in the antiterrorist cause."

SPC reports that she's been threatened on the street but hasn't been personally attacked (though other people she knows have). Of her father's killers, one was killed in the street, one was sent to jail for 15 years, one is hiding out in France. Their motive was to attack the representative (her father) of the Spanish government in the Basque country. SPC's friends have also been attacked by terrorists; one fellow worker was killed, another shot in a bar in San Sebastian in 2002 by ETA because he was active in "Basta Ya" (*Stop Now*), an antiterrorist group.

SPC claims that she has no nightmares, but does have flashbacks, as well as dreams about her father being killed. She doesn't feel safe. But she believes there is a nonviolent way for ETA to pursue its political goals, namely, through independent political parties.

"*Terrorism (in general) is repulsive, a practice of absolute power, in their means (torture and threats) and goals,*" according to this practicing lawyer and journalist. SPC says, she "doesn't know about God or an afterlife but leaves the door open." ("Such deep questions!" she exclaims.) Hers is a "*social struggle; terrorism is a crime against humanity.*"[14]

Accordingly, SPC thinks terrorists should get more than 20–30 years in prison. She says *she has felt terrified for 20 years*—a close friend's house was bombed, very close to her mother, and she lives in Madrid because "nobody knows I'm here and I don't have to have bodyguards." SPC concludes the interview by noting that many people, perhaps 15–18 percent of the total population of the Basque country, "accept terrorism, because in elections they write in the name of the outlawed ETA political party."[15]

SPC appears to have been terrorized and traumatized by the assassination of her father and by subsequent terrorist threats and attacks. But she is by no means immobilized or incapacitated—though her mind seems restless, her body agitated.

SPC's mode of living through her encounters with terror is in sharp contrast with other victims of "classical" "terrorism from below." Her body language displays her inner world in a way demonstrably different from other survivors.

In chapter 4, the variety of personal responses to similar terrifying experiences is considered in more detail. Now, I turn to a phenomenological account of the experiences of wartime survivors of the most common delivery system of political terror—aerial bombing.

BOMBED... FROM ABOVE...

More than a half-century before the terrorist attacks on civilians in Spain, World War II was raging in much of Europe. On the far eastern front of that war, in the Soviet Socialist Republic of Latvia, the war had started—but it didn't directly affect most local noncombatants until 1944, when a 12-year-old Latvian girl, "LA," living on a farm with her mother, three brothers, and a family servant, suddenly "heard airplanes flying overhead and saw Germans dropping bombs. But I have no bad memories of Germans, who gave the kids chocolate, played harmonicas, and didn't touch us. People freely collaborated with them."[16]

No one in LA's family was hurt or killed: "It's a miracle!" Her first memory of the bombing was when the front line came close to their home, which they abandoned. Russian airplanes bombed the German positions. "The noise was TERRIBLE! I feel my skin shrinking even now, the memory is so strong and I saw planes flying in the sky almost every day—was so terrible, like a scary movie, and you want to see it!"[17]

LA was afraid her mother or she might be killed. "I was scared and couldn't comprehend what was going on." They hid in a forest. Her last memory of bombing: "we had to leave our home, but we heard it and were so far away that we knew it couldn't hurt us anymore."

Regarding nightmares and flashbacks, at first LA said she didn't have them. But later in the interview, she confessed: "I felt scared by airplanes after the war and even today. Yes, the sound of airplanes upsets me. You know, I see and hear airplanes in my sleep, but you know it's only a dream and you wake up."[18] She held both Hitler and Stalin responsible for the war, as well as "all other leaders, not ordinary people, of course." For her, there was a nonviolent way to resolve the conflict. "War is terrible, thank God it's not here, it's the most terrible thing in the universe!" And then she spontaneously associated to terrorism, "You don't know the enemy; in war, you know the enemy. The terrorists could ride on the bus right next to you!"[19]

LA appears to have been moderately traumatized by the wartime bombing. She seems to cope by "putting disturbing memories and feelings" out of her consciousness, by evading and denying their power over her. As we will see, this is a common defense mechanism, one used by many people to distance themselves from unnerving images and sensations. These people have "adjusted" to a tumultuous and threatening external world by shutting it out of their consciousness. We shall return to this theme in chapter 4.

The second case study of a survivor of bombing "from above" is a Russian female, "RA," born in 1935, whom I interviewed in St. Petersburg, Russia, in October 2002. During World War II ("The Great Patriotic War" for all Russians), RA lived in Leningrad (aka St. Petersburg) with her "mama and babushka" (an affectionate term for grandmother). Her father served in the Red Army at the Japanese, French, and German fronts. He died in 1943 at the Leningrad front.

RA is an only child. Her mother was a shoemaker, who, during the 900-day blockade (September 1941–January 1944) of the city worked with a radio. "*War is terrifying*," RA declaims. Her first memory of that war is German airplanes' bombing of the city center in January, 1942. She was six to eight years old during the bombing and blockade, and felt "very anxious" the entire time. No one in her immediate family was hurt or killed in the city itself. But her cousin and uncle died at the front (as had her father), and some neighbors were killed by bombing.

RA's mother decided that the family should leave the city. They were on a train that was bombed, and her grandfather said: "If we're going to die, we'll die here" (about 30 km. from SP). She felt curious, not afraid, since she was with her mama and "baba" (granny) and reports having been interested in a screaming pig. But her mother suddenly decided they should return to Leningrad. So when they went back home, she thought, "If we're going to die, we'll die at home."

During the blockade, RA's family had ration cards for bread, ate kasha, had no heat, and made fires by burning books and furniture. "We were lucky." She says she saw no Germans during the war.

After a digression to her mother, RA claims no "special memory" about the end of war, but the end of the blockade for her meant that "My mother would bring me a bigger crust of bread." She believes that Hitler and Stalin were both responsible for the war. "*All humans are the same, no matter where.... No reason for war, no right to kill other people. Diplomats should have solved the problem, with agreements, not by war.... I don't understand war and I don't want to understand war. We need to find a better solution than war!*"[20]

RA reports having very strong religious (Russian Orthodox) beliefs, and she also believes in an afterlife, where the good are rewarded and the evil are punished. Her father was a local Communist Party organizer, and she, like many children of the party elite, was in *Komsomol* (the Party youth organization).

"All people need to live in peace," RA concludes. She exhibits minimal trauma or anxiety, and seems very mentally and physically healthy. Is this to be accounted for by the fact that RA was shielded from the most potentially traumatizing aspects of the war by her caregivers? Did her strong religious and political beliefs acts as buffers against trauma? Or is there something in her unique psycho-physiological constitution that insulates her and facilitates her adjustment to a threatening external world that has destabilized many of her peers?

"URB" is a 74-year-old Russian man living in Kiev. He was born in 1928, in a village in the Kaluga region of Russia near Moscow. His father and mother both worked on a collective farm, and he has an older sister. He says he is not religious and is apolitical. From 1928 to 1941, he went to school in the village.

URB's first memory of World War II was when the Red Army retreated from Smolensk. He recalls having no shoes, which was "very sad." On November 7, 1941, when he was 13, the Germans came, "smiling, with rosy cheeks." On January 1, 1942, the Germans retreated. Then the bombing started.

Initially, German planes dropped propaganda leaflets. Then URB's house was bombed, so he went to his relatives' home. He himself never saw combat, but did report seeing tanks and weapons after the war was over. "I was a little boy." When the war was almost over, he said he was a "partisan" because he helped get food for the villagers.

From 1942 to 1944, URB trained with the Red Army, but says he didn't serve in it. In 1944, his father was killed in Poland; "very patriotic," according to URB, and his father wrote "we are shooting the Germans."

URB didn't have the feeling he would be killed "because I was so young." His last memories of the war: "propaganda, crying, happy people, mother was sad (lost her husband), and I felt it's over, that's all." Both leaders, Hitler and Stalin, were responsible for the war, according to URB. The Germans came and killed children, bombed villages. Stalin was "a great organizer with no heart, like Bush and Hitler, all going to church." In his view, there was no way to stop Hitler without war, as Churchill did. "*War is stupidity...I'm against war...I don't need war at all and can live peacefully.*"[21]

After the war, URB read Solzhenitsyn's account of Stalin. "My father thought you have to work; if not you have to go to Siberia." He says his uncle was sent to a Gulag near Norilsk and died there at 55 years of age.[22] Regarding Stalin and the war, URB says*: "I praise him and I'm afraid of him...Very talented...Wrote perfect Russian. Our family was not touched by the regime, so I didn't hate him....I'm a very democratic guy and worker.*"[23] (Given his statement that an uncle died in a Gulag, it's difficult what to make of his claim that his "family was not touched by the regime.")

URB says he had no nightmares or flashbacks after the war, "*I was working so hard....Human beings double in war: they are happy but should be crying, and are singing and dancing when they should be shooting.*"[24] He says he has no belief in an afterlife or in good/evil. His tone is one of calm detachment, mixed with possible denial and repression, and with no detectable anxiety or trauma.

Like many Russian/Soviet men of his generation URB is ambivalent about "Papa" Stalin, but not about the end of the Soviet Union, which was "tragic" in the minds of many who fought for it during "The Great Patriotic War...."

"GG" is a German woman from Dresden who was born in 1927. Her father was an artisan, divorced from her mother. She is an only child, and a devout Protestant.

GG's father was a member of the Nazi Party—Hitler was the family hero! In 1938, she was going to school in Dresden. Her first memory of war was—September 1, 1939—while she was visiting her grandparents in Chemnitz. "The Poles attacked Germany," is how she remembers it....

She and her family lived in Dresden, but not in the center, until 1945. On February 13 and 14, 1945, Dresden was heavily bombed. Her family heard the air-raid alarm, left everything, and went to a shelter. Everything was bombed. "*I can never laugh again after what I saw and experienced. Then came the next wave—fire bombings. The asphalt was afire and I saw blackened corpses, which I can never forget.... Endless fire....*"[25] But no one in her family was hurt.

The next day, she walked through mounds of corpses. "*Thought I could die...and everyone thought 'This is our end.' Felt terrified...a Terror War...! The Americans bombed us to death and after the war gave us everything (to eat), treated us well, rescued us from starvation.*"[26]

GG's father was in the SA (*Sturmabteilung*) and didn't want to believe that Germany had lost the war. He was de-Nazified by the Russians, and then worked as a gravedigger. GG says she had no problems with the Russians in Eastern Germany, but had big problems with other Germans.

Like many Germans of her generation, GG says she had no knowledge of the concentration camps during the war, but adds that in 1945 she thought "*the Jews were responsible (for the war), but I didn't know any! I still think the Jews are the worst people I've met...! I wish the war would never happen again.*"[27]

GG is the only German I met who says she has a generally positive view of Hitler: "Der war der Mann" ("He was *the* man," for Germany at that time). In her view, while Hitler brought "order" to Germany, he also isolated Germany from the rest of Europe. "*We had a good life during the Third Reich! I wish for Hitler without war.*" The Germans were also *partly* responsible for the war, in GG's opinion, since "*Hitler could have thought more like a European.... War is the worst thing there is.... You are afraid of all people.*"[28]

According to GG, she didn't have nightmares, but "starts crying when she watches TV shows about the war" (flashbacks). She has very strong beliefs in heaven, hell, afterlife, and "God's grace."

GG is an unreconstructed Nazi, but is cheerful, even jovial, and appears psychologically quite sound...! While most Germans today verbally denounce Hitler and the Nazis, a considerable number still have fond memories of the period between 1933 and 1941, when they and/or their parents had work and were proud of Nazi economic and military accomplishments.

"DUC" is a Dutch female who was born 1923. Her family moved to Rotterdam in 1927. DUC's father was a diamond cutter whose politics "depended on business"; her mother was a housewife. Her father was Jewish, mother Christian, and she is an atheist. Both her mother and she are "apolitical." From 1927 to 1940, they lived in the center of Rotterdam.

DUC's first memory of war was when she was 17. She read about the German invasion of the Netherlands and says she "didn't know what to expect"; Dutch soldiers were all over town.

On May 14, 1940, the center was of Rotterdam was bombed. Dutch soldiers told her "*it would be dangerous. I was young, beautiful and went to another house. There was a hell of a noise. Of course we were afraid, but not as much as when the allies bombed later on . . . sounds of planes, bombs fell and destroyed my home. . . . Fire! Everything smelled terrible, smoke everywhere, wasn't able to breathe, everything was on fire!*"[29]

DUC went with her parents and neighbors to a cellar, where they stayed for one day. When they went outside, "everything was on fire, which raged a few days; terrible smell for weeks."

She says she didn't see anyone killed. The Germans came the same day, and DUC claims she wasn't afraid of Germans at the time. During the German occupation, she went to an aunt's home in Rotterdam that hadn't been bombed.

The allied bombing of Rotterdam lasted from 1941 to 1945. DUC says she was "*Glad when they flew over us.*" (She next told me about seeing a documentary about the bombing of Dresden.) "*Then I felt the same hate I had in the war then against the Germans. I was so surprised at myself and thought 'Good for you! You get the same that you did to us!'*"[30] (In her opinion, the fire bombing of Dresden was "justified" retaliation for the fire bombing of Rotterdam.)

DUC's (Jewish) father went underground and died at Treblinka in 1942, according to her mother. She says she wasn't afraid she'd be arrested, since she was (only . . .) half-Jewish. She hoped the Germans would lose the war and waited anxiously for the allies to arrive. "The allied bombing was worse (than the German) because you knew what would happen." She adds that the German bombing killed an uncle and cousin. She personally saw the bombs land and kill people. "*I was much more afraid that I might be killed but could do nothing except hide when the bombs fell. . . . Everybody was afraid. I trembled until they were gone. This went on for 4 years.*"[31]

Her last memory of the war? "Can't remember." The Liberation?— "You have to be there. I can't describe it." Canadians came in the spring of 1945. Germans were very quiet and took some time to leave. She claims to have had no problems with Germans or with the allies; she kissed the soldiers.

DUC knew the war was over from a BBC radio broadcast. "There was a horrible winter of 1944–45. I saw people dying, you couldn't do anything...you went on." She still has flashbacks, disturbing dreams, and nightmares: images of dead people in the streets, of people starving, of the crowd being thrown potatoes by the German soldiers.... "I was hurt inside because of the desperation." She describes her dreams as a mixture of hearing bombs and seeing the darkness. And DUC says her father, uncle, aunt, and cousin were betrayed by Dutch neighbors and sent to a concentration camp, where they all died.

DUC got married in 1945, when she was 21. Her husband went undercover. Hitler and the Germans were responsible for the war, in her opinion, "because they loved him so much." The Japanese were responsible for the war in Asia, especially for attacking Dutch Indonesia. But she doesn't blame the Russians—"too far away, and I was glad the Russians were an ally."

She concluded the interview by exclaiming: "I don't like war, of course, but there are times you have to fight, against Hitler; of course, there was no other way to stop Hitler than war." DUC expresses no belief in afterlife or in justice: "*The good are not rewarded and the bad are not punished*." She evidently has an acute anxiety disorder and moderately severe PTSD....

"EA" is an Englishwoman, whom I interviewed by phone from London in October 2002. She was born in 1909, so she was 93 years old (the oldest woman I interviewed and second oldest person) at the time of the interview.

EA is the oldest of four children, and she grew up in a semi-rural district. Her father worked in a shipyard; her mother made jam and was a homemaker. She was five years old at the start of World War I. During that war, EA had two young German acquaintances, who thought the war was horrible—one of whom was killed. She was part of a self-contained family unit, very distant from that war, with whom she had no direct contact.

After attending a teacher's training college, EA married in 1938. She was a primary school teacher at time of the start of World War II. Her first memory of that war was in September, 1940. She was at home, and the Germans bombed Leicester, the city in which she was then living.

EA says she heard the bombs fall and land very near her house—the top of the roof was destroyed. No one in her family was hurt, but an old man nearby was killed. *She heard the gasping sounds of two dying people, but she didn't think about it at the time—she says she was detached and curious to know about it, but claims that she wasn't afraid of death or anxious.*

EA's father died in 1941 of natural causes, her mother soon thereafter. The bombing didn't go on long then, but it did destroy Coventry, She says that *"A feeling of unease and of not being safe lasted the whole war, but as a philosophical person, I wasn't frightened....People were very friendly and cooperative during the war, we were 'keeping the homefires burning!'"*[32]

EA's husband was too old to serve in the war. Her last memory of the war? "Nothing particular, heard it on the radio." She didn't talk to her children about the war, which was a *"sense of strain. I was detached and had no nightmares about the bombing."*

Like most people in her country, EA believes there was no nonviolent way to have stopped Hitler "and his henchmen," but she doesn't blame the German people as a whole. *"The allies had no option but to fight fire with fire....War is an obscenity and an abomination, but sometimes it is the only option. I am aware of the real horrors of war....I don't know how to judge it, I leave that to people I trust, such as Churchill."*[33]

EA says she was never deeply involved in politics. "I was very Church of England, but influenced by Buddhism and Confucianism. I've wondered about that (an afterlife), but don't believe in a heaven or hell and don't know if the good are rewarded or the bad or punished....I was very lucky....I want to go out with a bang not a whimper!"

This calm, cheerful elderly English lady seems healthy and without evident trauma. She seems very distant from her experience, and perhaps that is a key factor in her makeup.

THE TORTURED AND CONFINED

ESA is a woman originally from El Salvador. She is now living in Ottawa, Canada. I conducted a phone interview with her in English. She was born on November 19, 1961, so she was 24 years old at the time of the attack in San Salvador. ESA's parents were both farmers and Roman Catholics—her father was an outspoken proponent of social justice and liberation theology, her mother more conservative. There were 11 siblings in all, 9 still alive; she's the youngest. ESA is a converted Baptist, and she says she shares the same politics (liberation theology) as her father.

During the 1980s, ESA demonstrated against the government, which killed, captured, and/or "disappeared" many friends and acquaintances.

On March 24, 1980, she was working in the cathedral with Archbishop Romero when he was killed by a death squad. In April 1980, a death squad, ostensibly looking for arms, came to her father's farm (where she lived) and took away her brother (who was released about two weeks later). She and her parents—who were "very scared"—were personally threatened, and were treated "like guerillas, although we weren't guerillas"—but says she "wasn't a bit scared." For the next six years, ESA she worked with a group of mothers to try to find "the disappeared" (men). On May 26, 1986, their office was bombed. She was abducted, blindfolded, and taken away by four men in a van. The men were sent by the police (government), said she was a guerilla, and wanted to know if she belonged to the FMLN (a resistance group, called "freedom" and "liberation" fighters by their supporters, and "Communists/terrorists" by the U.S-backed government and army).

ESA was scared she'd be killed, but she also claims that while she wasn't physically abused, she was nonetheless *psychologically tortured.* The Minister of the Army came to the place she was being held (she saw all their faces). She heard the screams of a man being tortured (electric shock) in the cell next to hers, and said "I was scared deep inside but I never showed it to them; I was very strong and confident." (She visualized the cell and the torture.)

According to ESA, this form of psychological torture went on for about two weeks. She didn't know exactly where she was, when she was visited by the Red Cross, to whom she "wrote a little note, which saved her," because it was delivered to the Baptist Church so she couldn't "disappear." She was then sent to a jail for political prisoners, where she had nine days of additional "mental torture," since she wasn't allowed to sleep.

After nine months of confinement, ESA was released in February 1987, as part of an exchange for naval officers. She emigrated to Canada the next month. She went back to El Salvador in 1992 and in 1996 but had trouble getting there because she couldn't get a U.S. transit visa (said the U.S. Embassy in Canada has her records).

ESA then mentions pictures she has of members of *COPPES* (Committee of Political Prisoners of El Salvador). "I can see their faces" (especially .a girl who was abused) and still has nightmares, "very bad dreams, crying...." She was in trauma therapy, and she "started to heal but couldn't talk about it for a long time...was in denial." Group support therapy helped. Sometimes she has flashbacks, especially when she sees movies.

ESA blames *both* the El Salvadoran and U.S. governments. She exclaims: "*Of course this was state terrorism/terror. You're suddenly denied your freedom . . . you're in a different world. . . . You never think it will happen to you. . . . This is a dream but it was really happening.*" She felt terrified during her confinement, "*especially when I heard the sound of boots, because you thought they were coming for you. . . . very frightening. . . .*" She believes in God and in an afterlife, and thinks that conscience punishes the "*ignorant, brainwashed soldiers, for whom one should show compassion.*" Perhaps surprisingly, ESA claims she doesn't blame them for what they did to her (and to thousands of other political prisoners and victims of state terrorism)— "*Everything happens for a reason, and there's a purpose to this life.*"[34]

War and terrorism make ESA "very sad." She doesn't want to see the news, since "the poorest people, children, and the elderly suffer. . . . We can ask God to clean the minds of the leaders and persuade them to change their ways. . . . Of course there's a nonviolent way to change these people's minds. . . . Maybe we can do something together, pray for leaders to change. . . ."[35]

ESA seems to have been severely traumatized and terrorized. The degree to which she remains so—despite religious consolation, social support, and therapy—is unclear, as is her prognosis. But unlike thousands of her peers, she escaped Central America with her life and limbs. She is the tip of the iceberg of Latin American survivors (and victims) of state terrorism.

"AG" is a male professor now living in New York. His father was an electrician and his mother a housewife, both Orthodox Jews, from Brooklyn. They were all New Deal—FDR Democrats. AG describes himself as having been a "good Yeshiva boy" until he was about 15–16. Now he is a nonpracticing Jew and a liberal Democrat.

In 1979, AG was working for the Voice of America, Central Asian desk, initially in Washington DC. In February of that year, he was a 35-year-old press attaché in the American Embassy in Teheran, Iran, when the embassy was attacked by "leftwing guerillas." The Ayatollah Khomeini's troops saved them. "We were all shot at." He didn't see people killed by the Fedayeen during this attack. Rocket-propelled grenades hit his office, and there were threats to blow up the embassy, which was surrounded. "*I was afraid I'd be executed . . . didn't have time to be afraid, and thought execution was inevitable. I was sure I would die that day . . . was on adrenalin, was busy and distracted . . . was sure this day would be the end of my life. . . .*" AG would live to see another, even worse, attack. . . .

By November 4, 1979, the shah had left Iran. The American Embassy was attacked that day by the Ayatollah Khomeini's student supporters. AG and the marines provided no resistance. He cried, was blindfolded, tied up, beaten up, but never tortured, although he was threatened (attackers put a gun to his head and said they'd kill him, but says he "didn't think the threat was credible"). "*The entire situation was a psychological beating... felt terror all the time: the fear was that you'd be killed at any time...felt it in my body...couldn't sleep....Was hyper-vigilant 24/7....I wanted to commit 'passive suicide.'* My adrenalin was way up, and I was depressed."

AG would spend 14 months in confinement—6 months in prison, the rest of the time in safe houses. On January 20, 1981, the day of President Ronald Reagan's inauguration, guards told AG he was going home, but he didn't believe it until they were outside Iranian airspace, when he felt elated. AG was one of 52 Americans freed that day. Of the entire group of hostages, none died during their captivity, but one of whom was medically evacuated.

Initially transported out of Iran to Algeria, AG was next sent to a hospital in Wiesbaden, Germany, and then back to Washington, D.C., where former president Carter met the group. President Carter seemed like "he really cared about us." But AG didn't care for President Reagan. In AG's view, his and his colleagues' liberation "was a deal, money for hostages."

AG is angry that the 1996 Terrorist Law doesn't apply to him and the other captives held hostage in Iran. For his ordeal, he holds many parties responsible: a succession of administrations on both sides of the American political fence; the U.S. intervention in 1953 and its support of the shah; the use of the Cold War by the United States, especially by President Carter, "who didn't follow-through on his professed human rights' values"; the shah's "corrupt regime"; and the students "who were simply following the Imams." His student captors are the only responsible party whom AG "forgives."

In AG's opinion, "The United States has a very skewed foreign policy." AG claims that he has had no nightmares or flashbacks, but he does biofeedback, "very little psychotherapy," and takes antidepressants. AG also says there could have been "a military solution that did not hurt Iranians," such as bombing the oil fields. "*I'm not for war, but there are 'good wars' (Afghanistan), and bad wars (Iraq)....*"

AG hopes that the good are rewarded, doesn't believe in an afterlife, and doesn't think the bad are punished. He says he "Was terrified but never suicidal" (in part because in 1979 he had two young children and a wife, about whom he was very concerned), but "hoped he'd die passively, that is, in an accident." He seems both resilient and depressed, a condition not atypical for captivity survivors.

"CHA" is a Chilean male who was born in 1932, and was 70 years old at the time of our phone interview in February 2003. On "the other September 11"—September 11, 1973—he was living in Santiago, Chile, where he was a cardiologist in charge of the coronary unit in the house of the then—president of Chile, Salvador Allende. Both his parents were pharmacists, and CHA has two sisters and two brothers, all still alive. He says he is a nonpracticing Catholic, and he has been a lifelong Socialist.

According to CHA, in 1973 there was "terrible polarization" in Chile between the government, which was led by the Radical (Socialist) Party, and the military (which was much more conservative and was supported by the United States). "The next coup was in the air, we knew it would come."

On September 11, 1973, CHA went to the hospital and then to the governmental palace. President Allende was on the second floor, and asked CHA for a cane, but CHA didn't treat Allende that day. CHA says he heard Allende's last words. . . .

Suddenly, the palace—an old building with thick walls—was attacked. There was a lot of noise and machine guns were firing; windows were shattered. CHA was afraid they would all be killed by the troops with machine guns. Then they were tear-gassed. . . . "The worst part was the dark, you couldn't breathe, anything could happen Then began the bombardment, but it was a lot less terrible than I thought it would be. Airplanes rocketed the palace. Then Allende decided to surrender. He took a white flag and went into a room alone, where he committed suicide. I saw him. . . ."[36]

Later, the soldiers machine—gunned 75 people, "I never thought I would be killed then, but I think differently now." Outside the palace, "I was more calm than other people, was hit in the chest with a machine gun, was freed about 6 PM and went home to see my wife. The machine gunning lasted into the night, watched the rest on television."[37]

A lot of CHA's friends were killed in prison. He himself stayed in Chile until 1977, then came to the United States to work at UCLA. Between 1973 and 1977, he "felt threatened all the time, friends disappeared,—it could happen to anyone." He was never arrested but was investigated. Colleagues were killed. "Yes, it was a civil war, the workers were armed but Allende asked them not to fire back. Allende decided to become a symbol."[38]

A coalition of police and political powers, supported by the United States, was to blame for the civil war, in CHA's view. "There is no doubt the US, under the CIA, instigated the coup. Allende was also partly to blame because he allowed into his government revolutionary Marxists, but it was impossible to defeat the military. A nonviolent solution was possible, but the US didn't want a political solution.... The war was unnecessary, but was due to US arrogance. But there are *just* wars, such as World War II. You have to look at each case. No real nightmares later.. for me it really didn't last, no real symptoms, just an episode in my life." (He then changed the subject to Allende.) But after 25 years, his "mourning was postponed until met a group of Chileans in Sweden in 2000, where I almost cried. Now I can talk more easily about it."[39]

This very articulate and well-educated physician seems to have "postponed" his mourning for a quarter century. He seems detached, even disengaged from the traumatic events that changed his life and that ended the lives of many of his friends and colleagues. Has he repressed his memories, or the powerful emotions accompanying them—and denied their impact—only to see them resurface? Is this a "successful" strategy for "coping" with terror and trauma? We shall return to this topic in chapter 4.

SURVIVING THE HOLOCAUST

"DUD" and "DUE" are Dutch Jews, husband and wife, and both are concentration camp survivors. In May 2003, I interviewed them at their home in Amsterdam.

In contrast with all other people I interviewed, DUD, the husband, asked me many questions about myself (wanted to know if I'm Jewish, etc.). He was born in 1922 in Austria, so he was 81 years old at the time of the interview.

During the 1920s, DUD's father was in Austria "due to World War I," and he was a printer, then "director of men's clothing, who started a boarding house." His mother was a *Hausfrau*. And his only sibling, a brother, died at age 27 during World War II (1943) because of illness.

DUD then started talking about his wife, who was sitting next to him. He said they were all "Liberal, practicing Reformed Jews." Upon return to the Netherlands from Austria, his father became president of a local Zionist community in Amsterdam, and he was active in the Dutch Labor–Liberal Parties. His mother was apolitical.

At the beginning of World War II, DUD was working for a German–Jewish refugee program, which informed Jews about German concentration camps, "*but couldn't imagine it would happen to us.*" (This may be a classic case of "denial.") DUD says he was "liberal" but sick of the *Volkerbund* (an extreme right-wing political party that supported the Nazis).

DUD's first memory of the war was in 1940, when he was 18. His father told him "the Germans are invading Holland. *We didn't feel personally threatened, we'll see what happens.*" In August 1940, a school was blown up but he "*didn't feel afraid yet, there's always anti-Semitism.*" DUD says someone started shooting at his house, and stone-throwing, but missed. In 1941, he met his wife in Amsterdam, and they married in 1942 (they are still together after 62 years!). "Full of unbelievable luck—we weren't caught and deported then with 400 other Jews. We were careful. We were frightened, but always able to escape (then)....We got a special certificate as newly weds, which saved our lives. We thought since we're Dutch, the Nazis wouldn't want to kill us."[40] (This sounds like a classic case of denial and delusional thinking, which was not uncommon among victims of political terror, and may have even abetted their survival.)

DUD thought he'd be sent to a work camp. So he says he faked having asthma and thus couldn't work. "I was scared to death, but a Gestapo officer said 'you don't have to go.'" He says his father paid a lot of money to get certificates for the family. In September 1943, they went underground, but, according to DUD, were betrayed by other Dutch. They were arrested and were told by the SS they could go free if they betrayed other Dutch Jews (DUD doesn't say how they replied...). He says "the others were tortured, but not us...."

In February 1944, he and his wife were sent to prison and then to Westerbork (an internment/transit camp for Dutch Jews, most of whom were later shipped to extermination camps). Two months later, they were both sent to Bergen-Belsen. DUD says he did "dirty work and got pneumonia" (he then showed photos of them together, and his wife showed me the Auschwitz ID number on her arm). "*Terrible. I realized I was dying and was almost dead. You don't accept the facts as they are; you're kidding yourself; afterwards you realize it.*"[41]

DUD's wife, "DUE," a 79-year-old fluent German speaker— which she says "saved my life"—then interjected that in Bergen-Belsen she fed and nursed DUD, but was caught in September 1944 (when she was 20 years old) smuggling food and was deported to Auschwitz. DUE said an SS officer told her: "Sie gehen nach Auschwitz. Haben Sie Angst?" ("You're going to Auschwitz. Are you afraid?")[42] She also says English planes bombed the camp....

DUE was in Auschwitz for only four days. "Everyone was afraid, but I was not...my luck was that I spoke German." She was with four other girls from Bergen-Belsen, two of whom were gassed, and then she was sent back to Bergen-Belsen: "*I didn't believe it! Told people there about Auschwitz, but people didn't believe me and didn't want to believe (what was happening) in Auschwitz.*"[43]

Her husband then interjected: "*The Dutch mentality is 'this won't happen to me.' We couldn't imagine what was happening in Auschwitz....We avoid the past.*" DUD says 1944–45 was a "terrible winter, no heat...then I was told 'your wife is back.'"

DUE says they lived separately in Bergen-Belsen, and that her husband almost died in a field hospital. She was liberated by the English army on March 23, 1945. There were thousands of the dead in the camp. The British put the Germans in the middle of the camp to have the survivors stone them. In an animated and proud tone, DUE claims: "I never did.... *There were three kinds of Jews in the camps:*

1. Non-attached (politically) Jews, who died like flies;
2. Ideological Zionists had a higher survival rate;
3. There is something else: Polish Zionists helped each other. I learned to be myself, to be Jewish, to look after other people. We were more Dutch than the Dutch."[44]

DUD then adds that they were put in a cattle car in April 1945, after the liberation of Western Germany. He had dysentery and was very weak. The train was bombed by the allies. At the time, he felt "*If I'm going to sleep, I don't want to wake up.*" The allies dropped pamphlets, which "gave me strength, the courage of disaster." He was liberated by the Russians. At that time, he weighed 32 (about 70 pounds) kilos, was sent to Liege by the Americans, then to Amsterdam. He was reunited with his wife in Eindhoven (Netherlands), and says she "looked like a child of 12 years."[45] DUE then says "I didn't want to live anymore. Thought my husband had died." He had tuberculosis and was ill for two years....

DUD says he knew the war was over by their liberation, but "it didn't mean too much to me. Let's wait and see. We have nothing to celebrate. I didn't know what had happened to my family."

DUE "felt (the end of the war) was too late. We Jews don't look backward but forward...After the war, no one in the Dutch government was helping us."

And DUD concludes the interview by declaring: "Egotism and self-interest, led by the state (and the *Volkerbund*), just taking care of yourself, were responsible for the war." (This may be ironic, given their prideful, self-reliant survivors' creed.) "The lack of responsibility by politicians and others (led to the war)."[46]

This Dutch couple appears to have been terrorized but not traumatized by their ordeals. Did they survive because of, or despite, such psychological factors as denial, isolation, and amour-propre? Perhaps pair-bond support. was also a significant factor in their ability to cope with extreme political terror.

"DUF" is a Dutch woman who was born in 1936. She has one brother, now 64 years old. Her father made window displays and had a textile shop. Her mother also worked in the shop. They were orthodox, nonpracticing Jews. She herself sometimes goes to the synagogue. She has "no politics, but father couldn't work after 1940."

DUF's first memory of World War II was in 1942, when she was six and had to wear a yellow star. She first attended a Christian nursery school, then a Jewish children's school. Her German grandparents lived upstairs from her family, but they were deported to Auschwitz later that year—and never heard from again.

While she was living at home in Amsterdam, DUF heard Germans shooting Dutch people on the street. Soon thereafter, her uncle and aunt were deported to the concentration camps: "they were happy to go, didn't know what was going to happen."

In June 1943, when DUF was seven years old, the Gestapo came and sent her and her parents in a closed cattle car to Westerbork. "I didn't know what was going on, but my parents were scared." They had no food. While in Westerbork, DUF was beaten once by a soldier with a leather club. Otherwise, she reports having seen no violence there.

The following winter, DUF and her immediate family were sent to Bergen-Belsen, "a special camp." Others, like her uncle, were sent to Auschwitz. She was "hungry all the time," saw people dying, starving. "*I was very scared it could happen to me.*"

DUF adds that she knew about the gas chambers. . . . She reports having to stay undressed for days. She claims there were no rapes, but the women were very frightened. "*Of course I thought I would die: Had to stand in line every day for bread, since I was the strongest of the whole family. . . . I was scared, terrified, the whole time, especially when in line, and I saw people shot as they were trying to escape. . . .* The KAPOs were terrible, both German and Dutch, and they were hated."

In April 1945, DUF and her parents were put on a train to Auschwitz. Her father said to a soldier, "Shoot me, not my son." They were in Auschwitz for a week. Then, on April 13, the Americans freed them, and the Germans fled. DUF was eight at the time, and her parents were very happy. Everyone had to go to a hospital, and her father had a heart attack.

During World War II, DUF never saw any fighting or bombing. After the war had ended, the Red Cross told her family what had happened at Auschwitz.

In DUF's opinion, Hitler, "a crazy man, was responsible [for the war]; he made the people believe he was right.... The allies and the Soviet Union knew, of course, what was happening to us, but we were glad they liberated us."

DUF had nightmares after the war, "not very often, but even now, about the camps." (At this point her husband came in and she stopped talking) "*I don't like wars; I hate wars—it's always innocent people who are the victims.... Very difficult to stop Hitler without a war he started.*"

DUF professes no belief in an afterlife. "Sometimes if you do good, you are rewarded: sometimes the evildoers are punished, but not often.... I'm glad I'm still alive." After the interview, as I was leaving, DUF declares: "*I hate all Germans; they knew.... It's a bad world. All this is still going on.... It was more than 60 years ago, but you never forget.*" DUF is still deeply scarred by her childhood trauma, and still angry at those she holds responsible....

"DUG" is a Dutch male, born in 1938, and a practicing architect. He was only two years old when the Nazi occupation of Holland began.

DUG has three sisters, two older, one younger, and five members of his family were deported to concentration camps. His father was a dentist, mother a housewife. They were all Orthodox, practicing, Mizrahi Jews and lived in South Amsterdam, near Anne Frank's house.

His first memory of World War II was the day his father brought home a grenade he'd found on the street. DUG claims there was a safe atmosphere at home and in his synagogue. He claims to have no real memory of Germans in Holland then (he was only two–three years old at the time), and says he heard about them but didn't see them.

In April 1941, he recalls that the family went to Nijmegen (Netherlands) and had to wear the yellow star. In January 1943, his younger sister was born. DUG doesn't recall anything about the train trip, but their deportation "reminded him of Exodus." He recalls turmoil: he didn't know what was going on. But he adds, "When there is war, you can also have false thoughts." Says he was "*curious, not afraid,*" and then, "*I am always afraid...maybe so afraid I don't remember anything that I tried not to see then.*"

When DUG was five, in January 1944, six members of his family were sent to Westerbork. DUG says he saw no violence in that camp but knew it wasn't safe. His father got them Peruvian passports. He recalls having been "very fearful," especially of "rough, proletarian Jews who would beat up 'civilized' Jews" (like his family...). He "imagined it could happen to you as well."

Later that month, the family was sent to Bergen-Belsen, "fearful, strange, boring surroundings...nothing happened." DUG claims the Germans were afraid of their bosses. He doesn't remember any violence, except for starvation, and he says he didn't see people die but knew they were dying. He had a flu and a high fever. On January 21, 1945, they were sent "on a nice Red Cross train" to Weingarten in South Germany (did he read about it or see it?).

"My memories are culinary. I didn't see any war: During a war, nobody sees nothing." (Is DUG in denial, avoiding what is painful, or mixing real and post-hoc fabricated memories?) He says he saw a dead Russian, but though it was a puppet. Weingarten was "very nice, clean, good food, saw people dying of overeating."

In February 1945, he was sent to an English school run by the Red Cross and then sent to Biberach, another small town in southern Germany. Three months later, they were, "liberated very late, by the French." He says he didn't see any violence, "nobody died in Germany then, except the Germans." All his immediate family survived, but were sick. But his father's relatives were gassed in Auschwitz and Sobibor. His last memory of war was when he knew (?) the French were bombing the *Hitler Jugend*—he heard American tanks and the Dutch national anthem. Adults told him the war was over.

DUG says he has no nightmares, but "sometimes I dream and daydream about what might happen to my kids if this would happen again. Where would we go? Not so easy to say who was responsible for the war. Versailles, Christianity, 6 million unemployed Germans in 1932. Allies made mistakes. Anti-Semitism. Is that cynical enough for you? War, I don't like it, I'm not a militarist, but sometimes it's necessary. My life was destroyed in war, but I'm alive because of the allies' war. Sometimes war is a necessary evil."[47]

DUG professes no belief in an afterlife (He asked me, "do you?")— "*I believe only in what I see and even that I don't believe in! I'm agnostic—this is not an Orthodox Jewish thought, but the bad are rewarded and the good are punished...this is the way how things are going... I'm a very good person and sometimes have seen bad people get rewarded.*" And DUG concludes by saying: "If you say you're a Holocaust survivor, people become guilty...*the border between normality and abnormality in life and war is very thin....The fact that people are bad and want to murder one another is more normal than we like to think...! I feel very terrorized, so fear is a normal feeling for me....Everyone in the world can be dangerous....That is what I learned in the war, even if I didn't see people die...The Germans were allowed to become sadists, based on my camp experience.... You are like them.... It can happen that normal, civilized people can also become murderers...If you remember that, then maybe it won't happen as often.... It can happen everywhere!"* He may be right....

THE WARRIORS

"BD" is a 92-year-old English male whom I interviewed, in person with his grandson. He is the only person I interviewed who asked me not to use his name.

BD's father was an inventor, his mother a housewife. He had a brother who died in childhood. Born a Baptist, BD converted to the Church of England. But he says he is now a pantheist: "God is everywhere."

BD describes himself as a "Very nonpolitical person, but I became a prominent figure in the Conservative Party." His first memory of World War I was when German Zeppelins bombed Croydon (near his home). About World War I, he says he doesn't remember much, except that his father was in the Royal Navy and was not injured.

During much of World War II, BD was on an antiaircraft cruiser in the Royal Navy. His ship was sent to guard the oil pipelines in Libya. German aircraft attacked the ship. In late 1940, "I sank two submarines and picked up the crews." BD says the German crew told him: "We would rather be British POW's than go back." BD claims he didn't feel "particularly threatened," but he frequently digressed, was evasive, and changed the subject.

During combat with the German navy, BD says his ship was bombed and his friends were killed. He himself was thrown 10–15 feet in the air, hurt his back, and is still injured (more than 60 years later). He was clearly uncomfortable discussing this, and changed the subject to card games.

BD's last memories of World War II involve his duties on a naval minesweeper, on which he served as deputy commanding officer. "I wanted to get home." BD says he "liked the Germans enough," and he showed me a letter in German from a German "friend." Once, on a destroyer, he says he was sent on a raid of a German radio station, and he had to shoot a German officer. "*It was a very unpleasant thing to do. He was going for his gun and I grabbed it before he did and shot him. I felt horrible, I hate killing people.... Killing a person is not on my personal agenda, but of course you had to do it. He would have done it to me.*"

Furthermore, BD claims that he doesn't recall the end of the war and says he had no dreams about the war. "*Hitler was an evil man and had to be contained. No nonviolent way to have stopped Hitler. We just did what we were told to do.... War is a stupid thing...for which there are sometimes nonviolent alternatives, but not with Hitler.*"

This was a most unusual interview. For one thing, BD claims not to have had nightmares, flashbacks, or other postwar problems. But his grandson—who was sitting next to BD during the entire time—said, "Grandfather, don't you remember that you told us after the war you had frequent nightmares?" Afterward, the grandson told me that his grandfather exhibited symptoms consistent with a diagnosis of PTSD. BD's credibility is thus somewhat in doubt. This indicates the importance of multiple sources of information to increase the reliability of an interviewee's statements, especially when the person being interviewed is a quite elderly war veteran who has had significant combat experience.

"GD" is a German male born in 1925 in East Prussia, near Königsberg (the city of the great German philosopher Immanuel Kant and now part of Russia). His father was a salesman and a "passive Nazi," and his mother a *Hausfrau*. GD had two brothers, one shot and one missing in Russia in 1944. He was in school until 1941, and then in the *Hitler Jugend (Hitler Youth Organization)*.

GD's first memory of World War II was his father saying: "That's a declaration of war on the entire world." He heard the radio broadcast of September 1, 1939, when Germany declared war on Poland, but "had no idea what that meant."

Soon thereafter, GD joined the *Waffen SS* and was in a tank in front of Leningrad. It was "horrible" (*grauenvoll*). He was cold and barefoot in the snow, but says he "had no fear that he could die, never thought about it." (This is a typical case of psychological denial and avoidance of the dangers of combat.) His SS commander said "You don't have the right stuff."

GD was then sent to Estonia. His mother reproached him for joining the *Waffen SS* (which is believed to have been responsible for many war crimes). He claims his parents were active in the Christian resistance to the Nazis, but that he himself at that time believed in doing his "duty" (*Pflicht*) and in "obedience" (*Gehorsam*) to his military superiors....

In July 1944, GD heard about the attack on Hitler and was afraid his brother had been involved. He broke his leg, was sent to a

German hospital, and was afraid he'd be shot by his comrades (who may have perceived him as a coward or deserter). GD was captured and spent the end of the war in a U.S. POW camp near Paderborn. He was severely wounded and felt "shitty." From 1945 to 1947 GD was in a U.S. prison but was not tried as a war criminal because lower-level SS people, like himself, weren't tried. Instead, he was used as a salesman in the PX by the U.S. Army. He was released in 1947 and went to Berlin.

During the war, GD claims he "*never thought he would die, did his duty, never felt guilty about what he did or saw.*"[48] He also says he didn't have nightmares right after the war, but in 1985 they started—he woke up one night and screamed "*Nazi Schwein!*" ("Nazi pig!"). He says he still has nightmares, about violence, but doesn't take medicine for that any more (adds that he has cancer now and has been lecturing about the war to German audiences—shows me some press clippings about his lectures).

According to GD, he is now "more Buddhist than Christian, doesn't believe in heaven/hell, but I know that life goes on... *I can't judge who's good or evil....Violence in war can never be justified....Put yourself in the other's shoes, people must learn to get along with dictators, as we did with Hitler.*"[49] GD concludes the interview by telling me about his public self-disclosures (as a former SS man), trip to Bosnia, work with Jews, and voyage on a Japanese peace ship. He appears still to be troubled by what he saw (and did...) during World War II, and is making an effort at "reparation."

"AF" is an American male who was born in 1923 and saw a lot of combat during World War II. I interviewed him in Sun City Center, Florida, where he has retired. He is quite active and gives talks to the public about his experiences during wartime.

AF has four younger brothers and one older sister, all still alive. His father was a weaver and clothing manufacturer, his mother a house-wife. A practicing Catholic and active Democrat, AF grew up in Newburgh, New York. He was in school until 1942, when, at age 19, he went into the U.S. Army.

While he was still in high school, AF studied the new war. At that time, he felt detached from it. He heard about Pearl Harbor on the radio and wondered what the future would be....

AF was sent with his army division to Europe. He saw the devastation wreaked by the Nazis, especially in Italy.

It was in Anzio that AF first saw combat. But before telling me about this, AF associated to: "psychiatrist asked me, 'what were you scared of?' I thought of combat....You were scared...." (uses the second person) "You weren't sure whether you survive or not."

He felt "great relief" after the initial bombardment and firefight and remembered "the noise" (bombs, firefights). (During the entire interview, almost two hours, AF was confused about dates.) "Hard to explain...Was a machine-gunner, sometimes saw the target, sometimes not." He saw combat in Italy from 1943 to 1944.

AF was comfortable talking about the details of his unit's march through Southern Europe, but was uncomfortable speaking in the first person, especially about what he did and saw. Even when prompted, he avoided talking about killing/dying—"If targets were available, you shot." (The constant use of "you" may indicate anxiety about killing, and consequent displacement and avoidance of personal agency and responsibility.) "Had no orders when to shoot, if you waited for an order, you died."[50]

During his march through Italy, AF says his unit was strafed by planes, but not bombed. He claims that no one to whom he was close was killed. In August 1944, while U.S. ships shelled German positions, his unit landed on the beach in the south of France. "You became supersensitive, the ears go up and you acquire a sixth sense." (Hyper-vigilance is an indicator of PTSD.) AF has confusing, non-linear, fragmented recollections and memories. He says he had very little contact with (French and German) civilians, but saw dead civilian bodies. He was constantly "concerned and apprehensive" but claims he never got wounded at the front (a claim that is undermined by subsequent recollections): "the battle at the Siegfried Line was not as bad as I thought it would be .... You don't get to know too many people, not too many friends."

In January 1945, AF says he was hit by shrapnel in the head, and was bloodied, His helmet "saved my life....I thought I might be killed all the time, wasn't sure what was going to happened, but didn't want to get killed in a strange outfit." AF also claims he "felt no difference after he was wounded".

His unit entered Germany in February 1945. The U.S. Air Force bombed the Germans, but no there was the Luftwaffe counterattack, according to AF. They went to Aschaffenburg and then to Nuremberg. "*No difference between them and us, the blood is just as red!*"

In March 1945, AF was one of the first GIs to enter the notorious concentration camp Dachau.[51] He says he didn't know what a concentration camp was until then. "*An unbelievable scene, mutilated bodies were stacked up everywhere.... You were beside yourself. How could anyone be so inhuman?*" He then showed me two black-and-white photos taken by his friend of corpses and skeletons in Dachau, which his company "liberated." He says he has no idea why the Nazis did this. His last memory of combat was street fighting in Munich, where he was in a ditch and heard 40 mm. shells falling. (He then showed me a photo of a German jet and said a German jet strafed him/his company.) In May 1945, in Munich, the fighting stopped. He was told the Germans had surrendered, but "there wasn't a word said, no hurrahs, just quiet.... We were silently content, thankful we were alive and in one piece.... My combat days were over, and Patton took over...." Later, he heard the atomic bomb had been dropped, and was thankful—because his division was scheduled to go to Japan.

Did AF have nightmares and flashbacks? Long pause, then he starts crying...and finally says he had *terrible* dreams when he got home. His mother told him, "You're not fit to live like this." AF then claims he still gets angry and feels guilty—and he hasn't talked much about it since the war. "*I didn't come out of my shell to talk about it until 4–5 years ago.... We men are not as tough as everyone thinks we are... just human.*" He still has nightmares and flashbacks. Then he associates to the war in Iraq, "which is driving all combatants up the wall." He says he was sent to a psychiatrist. He couldn't "stop shaking, and is knocked out when he hears a noise, sends a chill up my spine, after 58 years...I was scared I was losing it." AF says he has no idea "what triggers it...*it's right under the surface of your skin; it doesn't leave you.*"

"*War in general is useless, what a waste of time and men. What do we gain? What have we learnt? Nothing. We're destined to make the same mistakes we did before.*"[52]

Regarding World War II, AF thinks the United States "should have gone in earlier....With 20/20 hindsight we should have stopped it earlier....Hitler was mostly responsible...and 'the German psyche'... and Japanese warmongers." AF doesn't know if there is a nonviolent alternative to war. "I'm glad we used the atomic bomb. How would you like to be the first wave of soldiers into Japan? We knew it was going to be us...but we should never have gone into Iraq...a tiger by the tail, like Korea."[53]

A devout Catholic, AF believes in an afterlife, heaven/hell, and "yes, the good are rewarded and the bad punished.... But Hitler might have truly repented." His belief and support system did not prevent AF from being acutely traumatized by what he saw (and did?) during World War II.... He is the quintessential bearer of the wounds of war, most acutely "shell shock...."

"RLA" is a Russian/Latvian man, born in 1926, in the Kursk District of Russia. He had five sisters and three brothers. They lived on a collective farm with his father (a farmer) and mother. While raised in the Russian Orthodox faith, he says he is a nonbeliever.

RLA's first memory of World War II was when he was in seventh grade (age 15) and heard about the war from a speech by Molotov (who held many powerful positions in the Soviet Union and was a close associate of Stalin) on the radio on June 22, 1941, the day Hitler invaded the USSR. His 30-year-old brother was captured by the Germans near Smolensk, but escaped. No family members were killed during the war, except for his eldest sister's husband.

His recollection of the first bombing attack: "*My hair stood up from fear and I felt nothing. I lost my senses and felt empty. I had no understanding of what was happening. I was worrying about friends but had very little fear for myself.*" The air-raid sirens went off just before German airplanes bombed his village at night—the Germans used rockets that lit up everything and were dropped on parachutes. "*Very frightening.... Why did the Nazis have to bomb my little village? I saw many dead and injured people, and I had to take care of them. I was shaking it was so dreadful, but you don't think about dying because you drink a lot of vodka.*"[54]

RLA says he was injured during a German attack and showed me a scar from a bullet that scraped his face. "*No one cared about people, only about war.... In war, no one paid attention to such little things.*" His sister was taken to Germany, was sterilized by Nazis, and returned, childless. He worked on the farm during the war, but "can't explain how we survived" (he ate grass!).

At 17, RLA joined the Red Army. From 1943 to 1945, he was in the battles of Kursk and Smolensk, but couldn't fight and was evacuated and walked east about 1,000 km. After the siege of Leningrad, he was sent to Riga, which was heavily bombed. "Who knows how many people were killed?" *He became a sniper in the Red Army and shot many* Germans, *but "I couldn't see them."* (He was defensive and evasive about talking about killing Germans.) Then he showed photos of family. His last memory of the war was on May 8–9 in Riga, "a sunny day," when saw the Germans leave and felt happy.

From 1948 to 1952, RLA guarded the newly installed (by the Russians) Latvian Government. Shortly thereafter, *he says he became... one of Stalin's body guards, because of his reputation as a sniper* ("Comrade Kalashnikov" was a nickname).

RLA says he has no strong political beliefs or religious beliefs, and "I don't believe in an afterlife—*No one comes back.*" He blames Hitler and the Germans for the war, as well as Stalin, "both responsible—Stalin misused the army and killed the best generals." There was no nonviolent way to stop Hitler.

RLA is still plagued by nightmares: "*Not only dreams but I had to fight with the Russians against the Latvians and I can't tell how long I had nightmares.*" Even today he sometimes has flashbacks "*You can't forget.... Friends dying before my eyes, torn to pieces. I don't want any-one to see the same things and experience the same fear, but this was also the best time of my life.... War is FEAR.*" He pauses, sighs, and digresses. "Germans are the same people as we, not all Germans are bad." Then he shows photos. "*What is War? The continuation of pol-itics by other means*" *(cites Clausewitz).* "*Politicians are to blame for wars, who else?... Stalin did many good things but people feared him. At least there was some order, unlike today!*"

RLA is another classic victim of war-induced PTSD. He "copes" with his inner demons through alcoholism. And he apologizes for having cried....

"EB," in an Englishman born in 1922. He now lives in Bromley (just southeast of London). His mother was a homemaker, his father a clerk. He is an only child and was in school until 1939.

EB's first memory of war was on September 3, 1939, when he heard a radio announcement by Churchill. His first memory of bombing was in September 1940, when he was in London....

At that time, the German air force was making daylight raids on English cities. EB tried to "keep out of the way of the falling bombs." He says he didn't see anything but heard the explosions. He also claims he didn't see anyone killed by the bombs, but "I felt person-ally at risk and might well have been killed. You slept in the shelters in the tube stations."

EB joined the RAF at the end of 1941. He went on bombing raids of Hamburg, Berlin, Leverkusen, and the Ruhr in a Halifax bomber with a crew of seven. In August 1943, his plane was shot down over Germany. EB says everyone in his crew was killed except for himself and the pilot. He landed in a tree and was caught by the Germans but was not ill-treated when he was interviewed at Luftwaffe headquarters.

In October 1943, EB was sent to *Stalag* 3 on the Polish border. "Time lost all sense." He says he escaped from this POW camp on March 23, 1944. But he was caught again, and confined in another *Stalag* until December 1944. Germans marched him to Bremen, where he remained until April 1945. EB says he was very ill there, but was freed by the British RAF.

EB's last memory of the war was in London, where he celebrated VE Day. His last memory of bombing was as a perpetrator: his plane dropped bombs on Berlin....

EB says he has frequent dreams about the war, even now. These include nightmares; and he feels disoriented—asking himself "where am I?"—when he sees war films. He claims to have had "*No compunction about what we did, the bombing. We had no defenses against the German bombing. The only way to win the war was bombing Germany, which I did very effectively from 1942 on.*"[55] Perhaps he is in denial about what he (and many others on all sides "who were just following orders...") felt and perhaps he feels (still unconscious) guilt over his actions. Perhaps not....

In any event, EB believes that Hitler and the Germans who followed him were responsible for the war. "Hitler was a very good civilian leader but was mentally deranged." In his view, Japan was also responsible for the war, Italy less so.

EB claims to have neither political nor religious convictions. But he was in the Church of England. He professes no belief in an afterlife, but he does believe the good are rewarded and that many bad deeds, not all, are punished.

EB concluded the interview by saying: "*I was a POW, and if I hadn't escaped and if Germany had won the war, I would have been tried by the Germans as a war criminal, and I would have claimed I was 'just following orders.'...Sadly, war is a necessity that occurs from time to time because there is no alternative to control the actions of a nation or a group of people. War will continue, sadly.*"[56]

EB is *both* a victim *and* a perpetrator. Like most warriors and decision-makers, EB seems to have a realistic *political* appraisal of his actions, but little explicit understanding of the ethics or psychology underlying them. This a major reason why war is continuing, sadly.

On a Beautiful September Day...

More than a half-century after the end of World War II, it was a sparkling clear mid-September morning in New York City. A young psychology graduate student, "AC," suddenly flashed on the very real "possibility of my life being taken away." He was near the World Trade Center in New York City on September 11, 2001, "a beautiful September day...."

On that morning, AC was about 1.5 blocks from the WTC when he felt his building shake. He didn't know what was happening. He looked outside and saw smoke above the buildings—"no one knew what was going on." Then he saw the two twin towers on fire—"curious, so clean and perfect, nothing horrible." He initially thought bombs had gone off. He didn't see the people fall from the towers and didn't think the buildings would collapse. "Felt helpless, gawking."

AC saw one horrified woman and if asked he could help her. Then "the ground shook like an earthquake—What the hell was it?" and he ran, saw smoke, and felt "surreal, like *The Bicycle Thief*." He had trouble breathing. The crowd was very panicky and in a frenzy, "*this was the first time I noticed my state of fear. I didn't know how things would go.... Then the buildings collapsed and were covered by smoke. Was in shock, amazement, 'I've got to keep my body moving'*" was what he constantly told himself.... [57]

The most frightening moment of the whole day for AC was when he had a clear view of the twin towers, one on fire and one had fallen down. Then the ground shook again, as the second tower collapsed. "*I will never forget that view.... When will this end? We were in shock and didn't know what would happen next. When I saw the WTC on fire, I saw his (Osama bin Laden's!?) face floating in the sky and had an image of his face, I knew it was a planned terrorist attack. I hope that evolution can end war.... Yes, I felt terrified when I saw the crowd running around me and felt paralyzed for one second on my bike.... The people who did it are likely to get away with it, but there is a price for your actions.*"[58]

AC does not believe in an afterlife. And his notion of justice is restricted to "*the ongoing reward of humanity.... This is a battle, not a war. There is a way to fight this battle without violence, reconciliation between the terrorists and their enemies: Why did you do this? What do you want? Should attempt reconciliation before large-scale international conflict, which enters a primordial level with its own logic.... War is inescapable and irrational.*"[59]

AC has the hope that one day humankind can evolve past war. While he exhibits some anxiety, there appears to be little if any trauma or terror. He is detached.... Is this a, perhaps *the*, key to maintaining equilibrium during and after a potentially terrifying experience?

Several miles farther uptown in Manhattan, a young woman American female, "AA," is in a midtown office, not her regular office near the WTC. AA was born in 1977, and was 24 years old on September 11, 2001. She has one brother, one sister, and a father and mother who work in finance and health care. AA is a practicing Catholic and believes in an afterlife. She describes herself as "strongly Democratic and peace activist." And she works in financial services.

On the morning of September 11, AA saw many people in the streets of midtown Manhattan, "a mass exodus trying to get out of the city." She also saw the smoke in lower Manhattan, "but never thought the WTC would collapse." She claims to have been "afraid for her colleagues downtown," especially when she saw the WTC on TV.

AA's most constant thought concerned her own survival—"how to get home ok and to stay calm"—but she "felt personally threatened, panicked, your heart was beating fast and it was very scary to feel that was actually attacking you."[60] She "was trying to keep calm," and "would have gone crazy because I knew something else—that you could be next." She says she didn't see the buildings collapse, but "felt in great danger."

While walking eastward (away from Manhattan) on the Queensborough Bridge, AA saw that "the towers are gone" and started to smell the smoke, "like burning oil...which was horrible, and the air had changed, but it may have been psychological." She says she was in a state of disbelief and was crying. No one she knew directly died, but many people in a WTC firm she knew, Cantor Fitzgerald, were—"friends of friends."

"It was crazy. No one knew what was going to happen or if it would be safe. I started crying hysterically....It was like an atom bomb had gone off in the city." AA didn't go back to work for two weeks. In her office near the WTC, some windows were blown out and she lost some personal items. She still has dreams about it, "but not nightmares" she claims, and fantasizes about the WTC "as a beautiful rebuilt memorial."

A week later, AA went to the site of the WTC, "I couldn't breathe because the smell was so bad, felt like a voyeur....Maybe I could have helped them there, still feel that way. I should have been there; I wish I had been there with everyone."[61] This recalls the "survivor's guilt" reportedly experienced by many people who outlived friends and relatives who were victims of accidents, disasters, terrorist attacks, and concentration camps.

AA says she was worried about other people, as well as about what might happen next. And she reports having visions of people falling from the towers and of visualizing (imagining) her coworkers' panic. AA now thinks Osama bin Laden did it, but has a "hard time believing that any one person could be responsible....I really don't know how it could have happened...."[62]

AA has a strong view about what should be done. She is convinced that the response of the United States toward terrorism should *not* be a *"war against terror, but a military response for solving problems between states. The United States should deal with terrorism not through killing people or bombing or making others suffer....If you want to destroy terrorism, you have to look at all the reasons for terrorists and terrorism. There should only be a nonviolent response to terrorism.*"[63]

Although she is a believing Catholic, AA initially says she doesn't think the good are rewarded and bad are punished. "The soul is eternal," she starts, then changes her mind and says "yes, you are rewarded for leading a good life, but am not sure about punishment. The only judge is God."

AA admits she was terrified, especially by the smoke, which penetrated everything for two–three days, and was coughing for a week later. She appears to have been quite traumatized by what she sensed on September 11, and survivor's guilt may intensify her feelings.

"EC" is an English female who works as an artist and has been living near the World Trade Center in New York. She was born in 1956 in London, so she was 44 years old on September 11, 2001. Her mother and father, a postman, are both from London. She has no siblings, nor strong religious or political beliefs.

On the morning of September 11, EC was riding her bike. She was accompanied by her boyfriend (AA) and another male friend. She glanced toward the WTC but didn't know what had happened. EC didn't think it was terrorism at first, "just a plane hitting the building. . . . I felt afraid—couldn't comprehend what was going on, unpredictable, didn't know what would happened, had to get out of the area."

EC heard a loud rumbling noise, then "saw a giant cloud of dust overtaking us. I shut down, just moved on, difficult to breathe, had to go with the crowd, then saw the second tower collapse" (long pause . . .) "and I didn't feel safe at all, had to get home. . . . I feel immensely lucky that I might have gone to the WTC and {if I had done so} would be dead, but we didn't go. . . . I didn't feel physically threatened that I myself might be killed didn't feel panic or terror (?), since I was far enough away from the WTC. *But I saw terrified people, how they looked, with an unknown quality to their face, a fixed look, no eye contact, screaming. . . .*"

EC reports she started having nightmares a couple of days later. These went on for about a month, and she says she didn't want to talk to anyone. She says she has had no flashbacks. "The news said 'Arab terrorists' did it." EC does not believe in an afterlife, and she thinks that "most evildoers are punished, but their victims are tragically lost. The attack on the WTC was *an act of war against the United States generally, but it depends on how you define 'war.' Not an 'act of terrorism.' War is futile, and [we] should try negotiations rather than war. There is no justification for the use of violence between states.*"

EC's response to the attack, and her description of her subsequent feelings and behavior, fit the profile of the quintessential survivor of potentially traumatizing events. She appears to have been temporarily upset and mildly traumatized. But her symptoms seem to have gradually dissipated. She also appears to have had significant social support. How EC would have responded had she been in the WTC itself is open to question, as are the prospects for deeper and longer-lasting trauma should she (and millions of others...) be affected by another potentially traumatizing event.

"AD" is an American male, who was 53 years old when he was in the WTC on September 11, 2001. He is a practicing Catholic and works as a construction (formerly a nuclear) engineer. His father worked in a manufacturing plant, mother a housewife, both practicing Catholics. AA is the eldest of five children and describes himself as politically "independent" and interested in local politics.

On September 11, 2001, at about 8:45 AM, AD was working high up in WTC 2, the northeast corner, when he heard a loud jet engine, "a deafening sound." He saw a fireball and said "holy shit!" There were holes in the building and a fire. (AD had been in the WTC during the previous terrorist attack, in February 1993, but had left the building before the attack, and no one he knew was hurt then.)

AD took an elevator to the seventy-eighth floor. He was "not scared yet but some people were scared." He saw some people jumping out of the windows. He left the WTC, and saw its north side blow out. Then he heard the explosion, went to the subway took it to 34th street, "It was not a place to be."

Then he heard the first tower fall, and saw smoke rising into a "cloud." "It was unreal...Let me just get away from here, it didn't feel right...Saw the fire as I glanced back." AD says he was "not surprised, but saddened (by the attack)....When the second plane hit it, I had to get out of there, but I didn't fear for my own life...not calm, but agitated." He had led thirteen people from his office downstairs to safety.

To AD, the attack on the World Trade Center was "a *terrible, unfathomable, cowardly act....How can death be profitable to life...? This (attack) does go against all the order in the world....Not a war, but a war against Israel, that won't stop... but the United States is conducting a world war against terrorism....Preemptive strikes are not the answer....There is a nonviolent solution—to solve the Middle East problem....War is never a good solution....History shows that every weapon system ever created will be used.*"[64]

AD also says he's "dabbled" in nuclear energy, which "can't be harnessed reliably.... *War was a necessary evil before, but not now... world has gotten smaller... we have to live together.*" He believes in an afterlife, but "not quite" that the good are rewarded and the bad are punished, which "faith tells me." AD claims that he "never felt terrified himself, but saw terrified people screaming and running for their lives.... We were very lucky... My hero was the pilot of the first plane... he saved my life by hitting below my office... I had a 50/50 chance of getting out."[65]

At the conclusion of the interview, AD claimed that he had no nightmares, but has had flashbacks about the loss of life in the WTC. His everyday assumptions have been called into question, a theme to be developed in chapter 4. He seems to have very mild trauma (evident in the continuing flashbacks), but is detached from the experiences he has twice had in what was once the "financial center of the world...." Perhaps the power of faith has also helped insulate him; perhaps there is something in his character that has buffered him from severe trauma.

Why do AD and AC (the male graduate student) seem to have come away from the World Trade Center attack relatively unscathed, whereas many others (including AA, the female financial services worker who was not at "Ground Zero") are *still* traumatized by what they saw, heard, smelled, and felt on that "beautiful September morning?" Why do *some* victims of political terror endure lifelong traumatization, and others appear to "adjust" to whatever environment in which they find themselves (including Auschwitz)? And what do these survivors' recollections, experiences, and inner worlds have to tell us about them, and about *us*? It is to these questions that I now turn.

profusely and have other psychosomatic and neurobiological kers." They may attempt (unsuccessfully) to "fight" or ward off acute fear, or may try to flee from the perceived threat. But they lly do so in vain, since sooner or later they are tossed back into anxiety-inducing *inner* world, a character-structure (or "disorder," sychopathological parlance[4]) that may be temporarily evaded (via gs, sex, alcohol, combat, or some other intoxicant . . .) but is rarely ercome."

Terror, on the other hand, while initially experienced as a state of te anxiety, may be perceived by a terrified person to be of *indefi-* duration, and is endured in the face of what is usually a known, ble, and all-too-real threat to one's existence. Terror is more ense than "neurotic" anxiety. And the terrified, unlike people who merely afraid, feel themselves incapable of either "flight or ht"—they are immobilized.

A terrifying experience may open a pathway into the repressed, conscious zone of "basic" or "annihilation anxiety," a mental state which the person feels their very existence is threatened.[5] But while rror is a portal into this "existential" anxiety, it is identical with neither urotic nor basic anxiety.

Terror may or may not lead to trauma, an "internal breach or dam-ge to existing mental structures" in which "the predominant emo-onal experience is intense fear and anxiety."[6] While an anxious person usually more likely to become terrified—during and/or after a ter-orist attack for example—than a person without a preexisting "anxiety isorder," it is unclear why and how a terrified person does or does not become traumatized. This is in part because of the paucity of scholarly or even popular!) literature on terror—which is synonymous neither with anxiety (though a preexisting anxiety "disorder" *may intensify* a terrifying experience) nor with trauma (though a single, or repeated, experience of terrifying intensity *may or may not* induce trauma).

There is also the possibility that—precisely because terror is so threatening to our peace of mind and may so radically call into question our most basic (optimistic) assumptions about the world, other people, and our own existence—the very topic is avoided rather than investigated, even by scholars. Accordingly, terror is quite literally "terror incognita . . . ." In any event, our understanding of acute states of mental anguish—of which terror is perhaps the most neglected—is at best rudimentary and is very much a "work in progress."

Trauma may or may not result from terror. While virtually all trauma-inducing experiences involve extreme stress and terror, not all terrified people become traumatized.[7]

4

SURVIVING THE UNENDUR[...]
COPING, AND FAILING TO C[...]
WITH TERROR

The responses of survivors to extreme life events tell u[...]
about our common human needs, capacities, and illusions[...]
life events involve reactions at life's extremes. By understa[...]
we learn about ourselves, victim and nonvictim alike, [...]
become aware of our greatest weaknesses and our surest [...]

Ronnie Ja[...]

Terror for me was an auditory process. I was terrified all [...]
had no words for it.

German Survivor of the Allied Bombing of Wurms [...]

FROM FEAR AND ANXIETY TO TERROR[...]
AND TRAUMA

We all feel afraid from time to time. Some of us may be nerv[...]
of the time, especially during times of acute stress. That is [...]
Fear is perhaps even a healthy response to *real* danger—ind[...]
to take appropriate self-protective measures; fear may there[...]
mote our security and survival. But if not skillfully managed, [...]
terror, and trauma, especially in extreme forms, may threat[...]
preserve, our very existence and that of our species.

Anxiety is different from fear, terror, and trauma, although [...]
anxiety is usually an essential feature of terror, and trauma may [...]
not follow a bout of intense anxiety or terror.[2] Anxiety *is intens*[...]
fright, and/or dread—usually of limited duration—of *some unk*[...]
unseen, usually internal threat, often "imaginary."[3] Anxious peopl[...]

"Trauma," which is derived from the Greek word for "wound," was initially used during the early twentieth century in the sense of a *psychological shock*, a sharp penetration of the elaborately constructed mechanisms of unconscious defenses of a person subjected to a sudden, unnerving, and horrifying jolt to their system. Trauma has also come to denote *severe physical injury*. For example, *Webster's New International Dictionary* defines trauma as: (1). "An injury or wound to a living body caused by the application of external force or violence," and, (2): "a psychological or emotional stress or blow that may produce disordered feelings or behavior."[8]

In his possibly most innovative (and controversial) "metapsychological" essay—"Beyond the Pleasure Principle" (1920)—Sigmund Freud described as "traumatic any excitations from outside which are powerful enough to break through the protective shield. . . . the concept of trauma necessarily implies a connection of this kind with a breach in an otherwise efficacious barrier against stimuli. Such an event as an external trauma is bound to provoke a disturbance on a very large scale in the functioning of the organism's energy and to set in motion every possible defensive measure. . . . In the case of the ordinary traumatic neuroses, two characteristics emerge prominently: first, that the chief weight in their causation seems to rest on the factor of surprise, of fright; and secondly, that a wound or injury inflicted simultaneously works as a rule *against* the development of a neurosis. 'Fright,' 'fear,' and anxiety are improperly used as synonymous expressions . . . . 'Anxiety' describes a particular state of expecting the danger or preparing for it, even though it may be an unknown one. 'Fear' requires a definite object of which to be afraid. 'Fright' however, is the name we give to the state a person gets into when he {or she} has run into a danger without being prepared for it; it emphasizes the factor of surprise. I do not believe that anxiety can produce a traumatic neurosis."[9]

But terror—for which the closest expressions in English are "extreme fright" or "stark fear"—*can* induce trauma. And if the trauma lasts longer than "normal" (e.g., possibly many years after the trauma-inducing, terrifying experience), it may become a "neurotic" (or even psychotic, as in paranoia) syndrome—namely, posttraumatic stress disorder (PTSD), possibly the most contentious and politically debated diagnostic term in the psychotherapeutic nosology.[10]

PTSD was adopted by the American Psychiatric Association in the 1980 edition of its *Diagnostic and Statistical Manual of Mental Disorders (DSM III)*. At that time, it seemed a plausible framework for assessing and treating the problems of people as diverse as victims of child abuse and of "war traumas"—formerly called "shell shock" and "combat neuroses"—especially psychologically disturbed American veterans of the Vietnam War. Since the 1990s, PTSD has become a political football to be tossed between skeptics ("scientific" psychologists and other critically minded human scientists and psychiatrists) and clinical practitioners (mostly within the American Psychological Association).

Like fear and anxiety, fright and dread, terror and trauma, PTSD is a *theoretical* term. All these nouns are used in ordinary language to refer to intense emotional experiences and mental states. Like all theoretical constructs, these terms are elusive and imprecise. And the states of mind and body they presume to specify are tricky to observe and difficult to measure.

But these conceptual and methodological difficulties should not deter us from attempting to describe the *experiences* of terrified and traumatized people. These descriptions are based on the victims' self-reports as well as on systematic (sometimes "clinical") observation of their verbal and nonverbal language. This procedure is an initial step toward understanding the reasons why people who are exposed to similar threats to their existence respond in a variety of ways to terrifying situations—including virtually all readers of this book. . . .

Most of us will be a trauma victim during our lives. The probability of a resident of the United States being in or observing a serious accident, natural disaster, physical or sexual assault, or other event involving the possibility of serious injury or death has been estimated at between 70 and 80 percent over the course of a lifetime.[11] And this figure *does not include* combat and torture casualties, or illness and death/dying from "natural" causes.[12]

There is a wide range of internal and behavioral responses to potentially traumatizing events. Some people are better able to respond to political (and other forms of) terror; others are literally driven mad or are "numbed" into insensitivity by their experiences.[13] And quite a few may be traumatized for days or weeks but do not evidence the "chronic" trauma characteristic of PTSD. In other words, just as there is a *continuum*—without precise boundary lines—*of frightening experiences* from fear to anxiety and terror, so there is a *spectrum of trauma*, ranging from transient and mild to chronic and severe PTSD.[14]

In order to consider the factors that may shield us from or increase the risk of trauma, let us undertake a brief phenomenological description of the terrified. . . .

A GROUP PORTRAIT OF THE TERRIFIED

Between February 2002 and December 2003, 52 victims and perpetrators of terrifying political attacks were interviewed, mostly in person or on the phone by myself without an interpreter.[15] Twenty-eight are women, and 24 are men. They come from 14 nations and represent 15 distinguishable ethnic groups.[16] At the time of the interviews, they ranged in age from 25 to 94; and at the time of the terrifying incident(s), they ranged in age from 2 to 44. Most people, however, were adolescents or young adults during their encounters with political terror.

The people I interviewed can be divided into two general groups—victims and warriors. Forty five people (28 females and 17 males) were exposed to varying lengths and degrees of politically induced terror, and six others (all males) were in combat, where they saw and/or committed significant acts of violence (one elderly Latvian male, who said he was in the SS, was mum about exactly what he did and saw during World War II, and so he was not included in the above total).

In addition, *all* the warriors I interviewed may also have been *victimized* by the violence they saw and/or committed, and they *all exhibit demonstrable signs of PTSD*. These combat veterans performed "dual roles," as perpetrators *and* victims of war-related political terror. And they have all paid a significant psychological (and in several instances physical) price for having served their countries during wartime. . . .

Of course, this is an extremely small sample of combat veterans, and no previous study of which I am aware indicates a PTSD rate of 100 percent. Nonetheless, Chris Hedges reports similar findings: "In the 1973 Arab-Israeli war, almost a third of all Israeli casualties were due to psychiatric causes, and the war lasted only a few weeks. A World War II study determined that after sixty days of continuous combat, 98 percent of all surviving soldiers will have become psychiatric casualties. They found that a common trait among the 2 percent who were able to endure sustained combat was a predisposition toward 'aggressive psychopathic personalities.' "[17] I also consider the "personality profiles" of "successful" and "unsuccessful" survivors of political terror.

Twenty seven of the other 45 interviewees are victims of state terror, or terrorism "from above." Nine are survivors of "classic" terrorist attacks "from below." Three spent time in involuntary confinement, where they may have been mentally and/or physically tortured.

And the other six are Dutch concentration camp survivors of the Holocaust.

The vast majority of terrorism survivors "from above" were terrorized by what was literally dropped on their towns and farms from above—bombs. So were six of the warriors, five of the victims of classical terrorism, and two of the Dutch concentration camp survivors (who also had the misfortune to have been in Rotterdam during the German firebombing of the center of that city). And to this day, they "hear" the bombs falling accompanied by the terrifying, whining noise of the "rockets" as they whizzed over their heads. . . .

To be subjected to an aerial or ground-based bombing or rocket attack is to have one's senses assaulted, and, in some cases, altered. It is said that the last sense we lose while we die is hearing. This appears also to be the sense that is most immediately and radically affected during a terrifying political attack.

Over two-thirds of all the people I interviewed commented on the horrible, maddening drone of the planes that flew over their heads and of the hellish whistles and earthshaking blasts of the bombs dropping and exploding near them. For example, a Latvian-Russian female bombing survivor exclaimed: "I just had to hear the noise of the explosives and my heart would stop when I heard that sound."[18] And a Czech woman who had the misfortune to have been near the center of Plzen when American dive-bombers attacked it in the winter of 1945, recollects how she "was terrified when her building and apartment were hit by U.S. bombs. Everybody was frozen while hearing the whistling of the bombs dropping on them, and were unable to run away."[19]

Many bombing survivors still wake up in the middle of the night having been stirred from their sleep by dreams of bombing. And others have daydreams (or flashbacks) that catch them unaware, often when they see films and television programs with images of war.[20]

Terrifying political attacks also dramatically impact our vision. Almost half of the interviewees commented on the ghastly things they saw, including "mounds of corpses," "crazed lions running through the center of Berlin," "the bodies of people and horses everywhere," "fires raging out of control," and "a mushroom cloud rising like a smoking volcano over Nagasaki."[21] While—from a considerable distance— there may be a kind of macabre or terrible "beauty" about atomic-bomb explosions and airplanes crashing into skyscrapers, there is nothing remotely pretty about the horrors visited upon living human beings on the ground who are the witting or "unintended" targets of "strategic bombing" or "holy war." Visual flashes of devastation and destruction dating back decades haunt the "inner eyes" of terrorism survivors to this day....[22]

Although taste, touch, and smell are not mentioned as often sight and sound, terrorism survivors do recall many specific instances of assaults on these senses as well. A Dutch woman who was in Rotterdam on May 14, 1940, when the German Luftwaffe firebombed her city said "there was a fire like hell, streets and houses burned...(I) was on a roof and smelled dead people, everything and everyone burning."[23]

Often, several senses and one's core personal identity (especially one's memory and ability to trust other people) are scarred by traumatizing wartime events, especially if they occur during early childhood. For example, a Russian lady who tried to escape from the center of Leningrad in June 1941, just before the blockade, described how she, as a five-year-old child "was left on a train that was bombed. I saw many people killed, and a woman burned to death....Very scary, very dirty...and papa died on the front...somewhere.... This war gave me pain and nothing else. I had no childhood because of this war....Was is a horror, a big evil...do everything to avoid it!"[24]

Hunger, starvation, extreme cold, ice, smoke, acrid fumes, and firestorms also traumatized many of the people I interviewed. This was especially true during the 900-day blockade and siege of Leningrad, when many people burned their own books to have some heat during the frigid winters, and others barely subsisted on food and water rations that did little to quell chronic hunger and acute thirst. And the 9/11 survivors I interviewed have the stench of the clouds of noxious smoke and the taste of the ashes that fell from the sky that day forever etched on their sensory recall.[25]

WHAT TERROR MEANS...HOW TERROR FEELS...

Based on my investigation and reading of the relevant scholarly and clinical literature—and as a spur to future research—I have reached the following provisional conclusions about terror and its impact on the terrified:

As I said in chapter 1, *the term "terror" denotes both a phenomenological experience of paralyzing, overwhelming, and ineffable mental anguish, as well as a behavioral response to a real or perceived life-threatening danger.* My analysis of ex-post facto (sometimes as much as 80 years after the events occurred) descriptions of terrifying experiences by people I have interviewed highlights the following factors common to virtually all terror survivors:

First, the experience is described as having been *overwhelming*. The people felt *helpless and completely vulnerable* during the time of the assault (mostly bombings by airplanes during war or car bombs during terrorist attacks).

Second, the victims described the situation as *uncontrollable, a time of loss of autonomy and surrender of self-control* to an often unseen, and always menacing, "other."

Third, the outcome of the event is universally depicted as *unknowable and unpredictable*—possibly leading to bodily injury and/or death—and the terror is felt to be of *indefinite if not infinite duration*.

Fourth, the salient subjective feeling is that of *acute anxiety*, sometimes *panic*, and the cognitive orientation is of *profound spatial/temporal disorientation*.

Fifth, the person experiences their body as *frozen, immobilized, and often paralyzed*, incapable of self-direction and mobility.

Finally, the *intensity* of the experience of terror is so great that most people find themselves unable to speak, and later are left wordless when they attempt verbally to describe it.

Terror is profoundly sensory (often auditory), and is pre- or post-verbal. The ineffability of terror is a complement to, and often a result of, the unspeakable horror(s) of war(s) and other acts of collective political violence (like torture, confinement, and genocide).

Terror and trauma are experienced as potentially lethal assaults on one's being-in-this-world, on one's integrity as an embodied ego, on one's sanity, on one's existence.... They force upon us the all-too-real possibility of our own death and disintegration, a prospect from which we normally flee via "bad faith" (Sartre) and "inauthentic being-in-the-world" (Heidegger). As Freud says, "We displayed an unmistakable tendency to 'shelve' death, to eliminate it from life. We tried to hush it up.... That is our own death of course. Our own death is indeed unimaginable, and whenever we make the attempt to imagine it we can perceive that we really survive as spectators.... at bottom no one believes in his own death...in the unconscious every one of us is convinced of his own immortality."[26] And Ernest Becker has argued that the fear, or "terror," of death is universal and all-consuming.[27]

The fear of violent death, as the English philosopher Thomas Hobbes and many other "political realists" have argued, is what induces us to surrender our absolute freedom to a sovereign authority whom we authorize to use any and every means necessary—including the infliction of violent death on our "enemies"—to safeguard us from a "state of nature" in which there is a perpetual "war of everyone against everyone." Therefore, both historically and psychodynamically, war, terror, the fear of violent death, and trauma are dialectically related.

But the damage done to wartime terror victims often persists long after official hostilities have ceased, and trauma-inducing terrifying experiences during peacetime may exacerbate the psychological wounds of war and combat. As Freud says, "...the war neuroses are (the) only traumatic neuroses, which..., occur in peace-time too, after terrifying experiences or severe accidents....In traumatic and war neuroses the ego is defending itself from a danger which threatens it from without or which is embodied in a shape assumed by the ego itself....In both cases the ego is afraid of being damaged—in the latter case by the libido and in the former case by external violence."[28] Narcissistic injury is potentially traumatic.

For all mental states and human qualities—from intelligence and beauty to anxiety and stress—there is a wide spectrum of experiences and perceptions, ranging from very low to very high, with most falling in the "moderate" range. Terror is no different. And the people I interviewed—in terms of their comparative vulnerability to terror or their relative resilience from potentially traumatizing political experiences— are distributed along a spectrum of terror and trauma.

THE SPECTRUM OF TERROR AND TRAUMA

Of the survivors of political terror from above whom I interviewed, a little more than half (14/27) exhibit moderately high or very high symptoms of terror and/or PTSD—about 60 percent of the females (11/18) and one-third of the males (3/9).[29] Among the concentration camp survivors, 2/3 (4/6) still exhibit discernible trauma (3 out of 4 female survivors, and 1 out of 2 males). Fifty-five percent (5/9) victims of terrorism from below (either 9/11/01 in Manhattan, or Spanish survivors of terrorist attacks) appear traumatized (*all* the females I interviewed, and no males...). And all three people who were involuntarily confined are still perceivably shaken. *Taken together, over 60 percent (32 of 51) of the people I interviewed who survived political terror still exhibit detectable signs of trauma, either mild or severe.*

It is also useful to distinguish between those terror victims who appear to have suffered *very intense bouts of terror and still appear to be highly traumatized* (10 people: 8 females—2 each from Germany,

Holland, and Spain, and one each from Russia and the United States; and two males—one Russian/Latvian and one American, both combat veterans), *and those survivors who exhibit quite low levels of terror and trauma* (7 people: 4 females—1 Dutch, 1 English, 1 Russian/Latvian, and 1 Ukrainian/Russian; and 3 males, 2 Ukrainian/Russians, and 1 Danish). Based on my analysis of the data—which I did *prior* to reading other studies done of terror victims and PTSD—there are (at least) 10 discernible factors that seem to predispose the people I interviewed toward, or buffer people against, intense terror and traumatization. I have ranked them in order of importance, with the first four factors appearing to be significantly (and perhaps surprisingly...) more determinative of the presence or absence of terror and trauma than the other variables.

Of Primary Importance are:

1. *Temperament/personality/character structure*. People with *preexisting* anxiety and/or depressive tendencies seem the *most vulnerable* to terror and PTSD.[30] In sharp contrast, people with what may be described as "obsessive-compulsive" characters (using such defensive mechanisms and related psychological styles as avoidance, extreme attention to detail, persistence, evasiveness, perfectionism, denial, projection, and repression) with "narcissistic" features (such as unusual self-absorption, grandiosity, superficial charm, manipulativeness, and extreme dedication to self-preservation) seem to have been the *least* terrorized and traumatized among the interviewees.[31] Sigmund Freud called this character structure "the narcissistic-obsessional libidinal type," and Freud also claimed that this "type represents the variation most valuable from the cultural standpoint, for it combines independence of external factors and regard for the requirements of conscience with the capacity for energetic action, and it reinforces the ego against the super-ego."[32] Furthermore, it is my observation that "narcissistic-obsessional types"—because of their devotion to self-protection and personal survival and due to their skill at utilizing the tools and people available in any environment, no matter how degraded, to survive and thrive—*are also* the most "successful" in acquiring wealth, power, and social influence in market capitalist and advanced industrial societies. Ego-centrism, or *amour-propre,* may be unusually self-interested, but it also may be a very useful survival skill.[33] However, it should be emphasized that such categorizations (in terms of possible character structure and psychopathology) are not meant to be exclusive

and rigid, but rather are designed to *provide an indication of the (largely unconscious) coping strategies* of the most and least traumatized victims of political terror. And it is also possible that obsessiveness and narcissism, both "normal" and "pathological," may be culturally bound if not entirely socially constructed.[34] This explanatory framework is also not meant to diminish the important role of *non*-psychological factors (such as bureaucracy, group pressure, greed, imperialism, political/military leadership, and obedience to authority) in the genesis and prevention of potentially traumatizing terror and violence.[35] In fact, as Erich Fromm argues, "The thesis that war" (and terrorism) "is caused by man's aggression is not only unrealistic but harmful. It detracts attention from the real causes and thus weakens the opposition to them.... The psychological problem lies ... not in the *causation* of war but in the question: What psychological factors *make war possible* even though they do not cause it?" My claim about temperament/personality/character structure is restricted to hypothesizing that a *necessary, but not sufficient,* condition for experiencing intense or mild terror, and for developing or resisting PTSD, is one's psychological makeup, which may also be a genetic/heredity-based characteristic for the commission of "good" or "evil" deeds.[36] Individual terror, like political terrorism and war, is inconceivable without a psychological component, but other dimensions of human activity—political, economic, social, biological, ideological, and cultural—are also required for causing, and understanding, complex human motivations, behaviors, institutions, and actions.

2. *Gender and ethnicity.* Females appear to be more vulnerable than males, and girls/young women from Hispanic (Spanish and Latin American) and Russian backgrounds appear to be the most vulnerable females. Studies cited earlier in this book also indicate the hypervulnerability of Hispanics to stress and trauma. I am unaware of any currently-existing plausible explanation for this apparent fact. Some hypotheses include the cultural permissibility and inculcation of public displays of strong emotion in Hispanic societies, and the anxiety-inducing childrearing practices of Hispanic immigrant women in Anglo-dominated societies (such as the United States and New York City, in particular). There may also be a constitutional/genetic factor at work.[37]

3. *Injuries and self and significant others.* If a person was wounded, severely ill, or had other severe physical hardships (hunger, cold, etc.),

and/or a close family member (especially a parent), friend, and/or colleague was injured or killed, this is likely to increase the risk of traumatization.

4. *The type of terror experience.* The most terrifying and potentially traumatizing experiences seem to be combat, confinement (with or without mental and/or physical torture), and close proximity to bomb explosions.

Of Secondary Importance are:

5. *The length of exposure to the source of terror. The longer* a person had to endure political terror, the more likely the person is, in general, to develop chronic PTSD.

6. *The age of exposure to the source of terror. The younger* a person is (after infancy) exposed to political terror, the more likely the person is, in general, to develop chronic PTSD.

7. *The presence, or absence, of significant social support, especially a female caregiver.* People who had strong care providers, especially during childhood and early adolescence, during and/or after an attack, seem less vulnerable to developing chronic PTSD than those without significant social support.

8. *A strong belief system, especially religious faith.* This seems to me a *mild* buffer against trauma for some Westerners. I do not know about people from other parts of the world. I have read and been told that strong political and or philosophical beliefs, such as Zionist/Socialist ideology for Holocaust survivors or "a meaningful and optimistic philosophy of life," may also be important, but I did not personally observe this in the people I interviewed.[38]

Of Marginal Importance are:

9. *Locus of control and assignment of responsibility for the attack.* Terror victims who appeared to have at least some control over what happened to them (such as being able to flee from a bombing zone) seemed somewhat better able to cope with the terrifying event than those who did not (such as concentration camp survivors and others who were confined). In addition, there may be a slight benefit to victims who assign responsibility/blame for the attack to a *foreign* agency

(most often "Hitler and the Nazis") than to their own government. Interestingly, most Americans and Spanish victims of TFB assigned *joint* responsibility for the attacks on them to al-Qaeda/ETA *and* to the U.S. or Spanish government, respectively, for failing to prevent the terrorist attack and/or for also failing to provide sufficient support after the attack. But no English or Dutch survivors of political terror blamed their own governments for what happened to them. Many survivors of World War II bombing attacks in the former Soviet Union tended to blame *both* the attacking air forces (German, American and/or British) *and* their own government for the war/attacks.

10. *Belief in "Justice," either in this world or in the afterlife.* Terror victims who believe that "the good are rewarded and the bad are punished," may do marginally better than those who do not. In addition, belief in an afterlife—including "hell" for the "wicked" and "heaven" for the "good"—may also be of marginal benefit to some survivors of terrifying political attacks.

The factors that intensify or mollify terrifying experiences are themselves rooted in even more fundamental, underlying features of our existence—the very preconditions for being human, all-too-human. These include but are not restricted to invariant features of cognition, such as language, memory, and perception. But they also repose upon a ground of human existence that sometimes motivates us to desire things we don't need, and to do things that may "feel good" at the time but which come back to haunt us, both individually and collectively. These motivators are sometimes called drives or instincts, and also include a limited set of universal emotions, "an affective ontology," of which fear and anger may be the most "basic," and the most base. . . .

BASIC "INSTINCTS": FEAR AND TERROR; ANGER, RAGE AND . . . REVENGE/RETALIATION?

Terror—or *intense fear* about personal disintegration and annihilation—and rage—or *intense anger* at an external object for allegedly posing a potentially mortal threat to anything one holds near and dear—appear to be, like our inclination toward self—preservation, publicly observable expressions of our most "basic instincts."[39] Neuroscientists such as Joseph LeDoux and Anthony Damasio are following not just Freud, but an ancient tradition, when they postulate the existence and influence of such "basic" or "primary" emotions as fear and anger.[40] For example, Confucius (or Kung-fu-tse) is cited as having asked: "What are the feelings of men? They are joy, anger, sadness, fear, love, liking, and disliking. These seven feelings do not have to be learned by men."[41] By focusing on such potentially "destructive instincts" as aggression and anger, Freud and more contemporary analysts of our dire condition are also "followers" of Confucian and other ancient traditions. Confucius is also reported to have said, "If a man be under the influence of anger his conduct will not be correct. The same will be the case if he be under the influence of terror…or of sorrow, or distress."[42] Little has changed over the millennia, except that there are now have thousands of weapons of global destruction to be deployed when those who possess them "feel" they "should" be used against their "enemies."

For about a century, Freud and other psychoanalysts and social theorists have tried to understand the universal, largely unconscious roots of war and violent human conflict. Partially as a result of his observations of the carnage of World War I, Freud postulated an "eternal struggle" between two transhistorical forces or "drives," *Eros* (or libido, the life-force) and *Thanatos* (or the death-drive), from which Freud believed "the aggressive instinct derived."[43] Wilhelm Reich, while agreeing with Freud on most issues, denied the existence of a death drive and instead focused on the healthy and pathological ways in which erotic energy, or "sexual economy," may be channeled. Reich, like Jung before him (though without what Reich called Jung's "mystification of the whole thing") rejected the duality of drives in general and of the existence of an autonomous death instinct in particular. Instead, Reich claimed that "all the many instincts we have—oral, anal, and so on—…have some common root….in a common biological principle."[44]

Melanie Klein and many of her "object-relations" followers, on the other hand, extended Freud's notion of a death drive and traced it all the way back to its alleged manifestations in our earliest infantile anxieties, frustrations, and acts of oral aggression, as well as to a "psychotic core" supposedly present in all human beings.[45] Proceeding from this assumption, the Italian psychoanalyst Franco Fornari, citing anthropological studies of tribes who seemed to have abolished war but nonetheless remained acutely afraid of death, argues that, "*the fear of annihilation* (which the idea of renouncing war arouses in man) *would appear to arise not so much from his being threatened by a real external danger* (i.e. from his being disarmed and therefore at the mercy of an external enemy), *as from the fact that he finds himself confronted by annihilation as a totally illusory danger connected with psychotic anxiety.*…What has been observed among primitive peoples deprived of war seems to constitute a decisive proof in favor of the Freudian theory of the death instinct, since it confronts us with the realm of destruction not as an exogenous situation, but as a purely endogenous emergence. . . . It seems to me . . . correct to say that both religion and war originate in the elaboration of psychotic anxieties connected with mourning and that each of them constitutes a social-ized mode of defense against such anxieties" (as with the sometimes paranoid-psychotic and sometimes realistic fear of annihilation).[46]

The great psychoanalytic theorist and popularizer Erich Fromm, on the other hand, like Wilhelm Reich, detected insurmountable dif-ficulties with Freud's notion of a death instinct, which Fromm spec-ulated may have been based on Freud's apparent preoccupation with his own death anxiety (*Todesangst*).[47] Regardless of the existence or non-existence of a death drive—and I personally do not think that a dichotomy between "life" and "death" instincts is scientifically or his-torically plausible—the virtually universal existence of violence and war inevitably leads one to speculate about the reasons for normal and extreme ("benign and malignant," in Fromm's formulation) human aggression. If socially directed outward, toward others, "malignant" aggression may take the forms of sadism, torture, war, and other forms of violent conflict, And if directed inward, the powerful psy-chosomatic energy we call aggression is experienced as masochism, depression, guilt, mourning, and self-hatred. In any event, war and terror—inner and outer—seem joined at the psychological hip.[48]

THE RIDDLES OF TERROR: QUESTIONS WITHOUT ANSWERS . . .

Among the unanswered (and possibly unanswerable . . .) riddles and questions raised by the virtually universal existence of war, terror, terrorism, and trauma are the following:

Is the source of terror primarily intrapsychic, some unresolved and possibly unresolvable unconscious conflict between repressed impulses and desires? Or is terror a situationally appropriate response to an externally induced, environmental cause, one that triggers overpow-ering feelings of dread and vulnerability? Perhaps terror is even deeper, an ontological affective condition of human existence, of our being-in-this-world—but a state of being most humans try to avoid most of their lives. . . .

What is terror's relation to aggression and violence? Does the inten-sity of the experience of terror unleash, and even rationalize, aggressive and violent responses to those we blame for our unbearable anxiety?

How do we behave when we feel terrified? Do we seek immediately and automatically to rid ourselves of terror? Do we then transmit this emotionally intolerable condition to others, whom we then brand as "terrorists," the alleged cause and source of our unease? Is terror contagious, spreading uncontrollably among panic-stricken people?

Does the unbearable heaviness of being in terror compel us to expel, split off, and dissociate terror, as quickly as possible and by any means necessary? How may terror be "managed"? Can terror be reduced, even eradicated, or is it a precondition for what it means to be (fully) human?

Are "terrorists" really "criminals," "fanatics," "evil," "zealots," wholly "other" to us? Or are they to a remarkable degree the "shadow side" of "civilized peoples," the unleashed and unrepressed violence lurking in virtually all of us? Do many "terrorists," especially those with deep ideological and/or religious convictions, have a way of facing death from which we might learn, even if we deplore their taking of human life?

Based on my reading of the extant psychological, psychoanalytic, historical, and social-scientific literature, as well as on a content analysis of more than 50 interviews I have conducted with survivors of terrifying political violence, I tentatively conclude: *We don't yet know the answers to these important questions!* This is in part because of the lack of good academic discourse on terror (except in relation to horror films and to PTSD). It is also due to the *overdetermined* and complex nature of terror, and of its important, but poorly understood, connections to anxiety, horror, panic, paralysis, and trauma, common to virtually all terror survivors.

It is to the common condition of all humanity—the "ground" upon which the individual tragic tales of terror and trauma are enacted—and the possible future(s) of our life on Earth, that I now turn to conclude this book.

CONCLUSION

IMAGINING THE UNIMAGINABLE?
A WORLD WITHOUT (OR WITH LESS . . .)
TERROR AND TERRORISM?

Say to yourself in the morning: I shall meet people who are interfering, ungracious, insolent, full of guile, deceitful, and antisocial. . . . But I . . . who know that the nature of the wrongdoer is of one kin with mine—not indeed of the same blood or seed but sharing the same kind, the same portion of the divine—I cannot be harmed by any one of them, and no one can involve me in shame. I cannot feel anger against him who is of my kin, nor hate him. . . . To work against one another is therefore contrary to nature, and to be angry against a man or turn one's back on him is to work against him. . . . The best method of defense is not to become like your enemy.[1]

Marcus Aurelius

You have heard that it was said, "An eye for an eye and a tooth for a tooth." But I say to you, offer no resistance to one who is evil. . . . You have heard that it was said, "You shall love your neighbor and hate your enemy." But I say to you, love your enemies, and pray for those who persecute you. . . . For if you love only those who love you, what recompense will you have?[2]

The New Testament

Against them make ready your strength to the utmost of your power, including steeds of war, to strike terror into (the hearts of) the enemies, of Allah and our enemies, and others besides, whom you may not know but whom Allah knows. . . . But if the enemy incline toward peace, you (also) incline toward peace, and trust in Allah. . . .[3]

The Qur'an

The ideal man was described (in the Talmud) as follows: "Those who are insulted but do not insult, hear their shame but do not reply, act out of love and rejoice in suffering, of them it was written: 'And those who love Him will be as the sun in its splendor.' "[4]

The Talmud

For hatred does not cease by hatred at any time: hatred ceases by love, this is an old rule. . . . The world does not know that we must all come to an end here;—but those who know it, their quarrels cease at once. . . . All men tremble at punishment, all men fear death; remember that you are like unto them, and do not kill, nor cause punishment. . . . Victory breeds hatred, for the conquered is unhappy. He who has given up both victory and defeat, he, the contented, is happy. . . . A man is not just if he carries a matter by violence; no, he who distinguishes both right and wrong, who is learned and leads others, not by violence, but by law and equity, and who is guarded by law and intelligent, he is called just.[5]

The Dhammapada

Wrath breeds stupefaction, stupefaction leads to loss of memory, loss of memory ruins the reason, and the ruin of reason spells utter destruction. . . . The Lord said: Non-violence, even-mindedness, contentment, austerity, beneficence, good and ill fame—all these various attributes of creatures proceed verily from me.[6]

Bhagavad-Gita

Mankind lives between two eternities, warring against oblivion.

Attributed to Confucius

If they (great nations) can shed the fear of destruction, if they disarm themselves, they will automatically help the rest to regain their sanity. But then these great powers will have to give up their imperialistic ambitions and their exploitation of the so-called uncivilized and semicivilized nations of the earth and revise their mode of life. It means a complete revolution.[7]

Mohandas K. Gandhi

As this chapter's opening citations may indicate, there is an apparent congruence (or to use Johann Wolfgang von Goethe's felicitous term, an "elective affinity") among the world's great spiritual and religious, pagan, and humanistic traditions regarding the most pressing, and contentious, issues of our history—justice, killing, enemies and enmity, destruction and divinity, peace, and virtue. But just as "the devil can cite scripture for his purposes," so can the pacifist. And another, more bellicose, writer might not be unduly challenged to find passages from the great classical, Muslim, Jewish, Christian, Buddhist, Hindu, and Confucian texts—even isolated passages penned by Gandhi[8]—to edify the martial virtues.

Still, there has been an emerging consensus among humankind's most distinguished scientists, scholars, and religious leaders that violence and war are rarely, if ever, justifiable, and that mega-war and mega-terrorism in the twenty-first century represent the greatest human-created threats to life on Earth in the history of our species. Sigmund Freud, perhaps the most influential (and misunderstood) explorer of the human psyche, and Albert Einstein, the quintessential framer of our contemporary scientific understanding of the universe as a whole, were in agreement about the pressing need for a radical and rapid transformation of international relations and the outdated thinking underlying it.

Albert Einstein—*Time* magazine's "Man of the Twentieth Century," in a private letter written in late 1931 or early 1932, commented to Freud that: "... there shines through the cogent logic of your arguments a deep longing for the great goal of internal and external liberation of mankind from war. This great aim has been professed by all those who have been venerated as moral and spiritual leaders ... from Jesus Christ to Goethe and Kant. Is it not significant that such men have been universally accepted as leaders, even though their efforts to mold the course of human affairs were attended with but such small success? *I am convinced that the great men ... have little influence on the course of political events. It almost looks as if this domain on which the fate of nations depends has inescapably to be given over to the violence and irresponsibility of political leaders.*"[9]

Later in 1932, Freud replied to Einstein in the classic missive "Why War?" "You begin with the relation between Right (*Recht*) and Might (*Macht*).... But may I replace the word 'might' by the balder and harsher word 'violence?' Today right and violence appears to us as antitheses.... It is a general principle, then, that conflicts of interest between men are settled by the use of violence.... Thus the result of all these warlike efforts has only been that the human race has exchanged numerous, and indeed unending, minor wars for wars on a grand scale that are rare but all the more destructive."[10]

The "War on Terrorism" is already a destructive conflict on a grand scale, one that might become planetary destruction unless nonviolent means are devised and implemented—soon—to address and resolve the legitimate and perceived grievances on *all* sides of this conflict.

Freud continues his letter to Einstein by warning that, "wars will only be prevented with certainty if mankind unites in setting up a central authority to which the right of giving judgment upon all conflicts of interest shall be handed over. There are clearly two separate requirements involved in this: the creation of a supreme authority and its endowment with the necessary power. One without the other would be useless."[11]

The United Nations was intended by some of its creators to be such an authority. However, due largely to the opposition of the "great" (aka nuclear) powers (most often the United States, followed by the former Soviet Union, China, France, and Great Britain, each of which has a veto in the Security Council), the United Nations has never had "the necessary power" to enforce the will of most of its "central authorities," especially the General Assembly. Until and unless the United Nations, or a more powerful successor, is accorded the "might" (peace*making* in addition to peacekeeping authority), it is likely that Freud's skepticism will be justified.

THE "MORALITY" OF TERRORISM

The history of mankind is a history of horrors.
                    Denys Arcand, "The Barbarian Invasions"

And is Man any the less destroying himself for all this boasted brain of his? . . . in the arts of death, he outdoes Nature herself, and produces by chemistry and machinery all the slaughter of plague, pestilence, and famine. . . . The highest form of literature is the tragedy, a play in which everyone is murdered at the end. . . . the power that governs the earth is not the power of Life but of Death; and the inner need that has nerved Life to the effort of organizing itself into the human being is not the need for higher life but for a more efficient engine of destruction. . . . Man, the inventor of the rack, the stake, the gallows, the electric chair; of sword and gun and poison gas; above all, of justice, duty, patriotism, and all the other isms by which even those who are clever enough to be humanely disposed are persuaded to become the most destructive of all the destroyers.[12]
                    The Devil, *Man and Superman*, Bernard Shaw

Since the beginning of recorded history, bloodcurdling and horrific accounts depicting the atrocities perpetrated by human beings (mostly but not exclusively adolescent and adult males) on their "enemies" (and sometimes, as in Greek tragedies, on their own families and friends) have been narrated (by Homer and his followers) and penned (from Virgil and Julius Caesar to Primo Levi and Alexander Solzhenitsyn). Many conventional history and political science texts read like a chronology of wars and conquests. The mass media are filled with sanitized images of slaughter and depredation. And the most prominent stories of modern times are headlined by attention-grabbing bites luring the casual observer into ravenously consuming texts and graphics about massacres, bombings, and the usually too-late and too-little efforts by diplomats and law enforcement agencies to stop the carnage and to apprehend the alleged perpetrators.

Consistent with their largely conformist role since the creation of the Cold War, American mass media have tended to "manufacture popular consent" to the Anglo-American "coalition's" packaging of "terrorism" and "the war against terror" as a millenarian struggle between the forces of freedom, democracy, and good ("us"), and the "barbarians and terrorists" who would destroy "our civilization."[13] The ancient Romans would have approved.

Terrorism may have begun as a political tool used by marauding bands and armies to intimidate, torture, and coerce their victims and adversaries into betraying confidences and cowing into submission. And as the history of the Roman Empire shows, imperious and imperial terrorism committed by an empire against those perceived as disloyal and seditious (from Jesus Christ and other Jewish "enemies of Rome," to Spartacus, the "barbarians," and early Christian communities) as often as not kindled the sparks of further rebellions and violent insurrections, some of which (like those catalyzed by the Zealots) used "targeted assassinations" against the Empire's representatives. This pattern of imperial domination via direct and structural terrorist violence from above, and piecemeal terrorist violence from below, continues to this day—and is as ethically (and legally) reprehensible now as it was two millennia ago.

My underlying assumption is that unless necessary and sufficient conditions can be provided by perpetrators of "terrorism from above" (i.e., state actors using "terror bombing" to attempt to break the morale of a civilian population and its government, as has been done many times since the Italians bombed Tripoli in 1911), and by "terrorists from below" (ranging from the Russian revolutionaries and defenders of "Red Terror" during the late nineteenth and early twentieth centuries to al-Qaeda) to justify their acts, *any* act that deliberately inculcates terror is, more or less, unethical.

However, there are *degrees* of moral culpability. The decisions by Churchill to target the civilian populations (especially the working-class neighborhoods of industrial cities) of Germany for "terror bombings" during World War II, and by Truman to "nuke" Hiroshima and Nagasaki (which had no military significance) are, by this criterion, acts of "terrorism from above." But they are not morally equivalent to such acts of "terrorism from below" as the terrorist attacks of September 11, 2001, on the United States, or of the acts of other terrorist groups (such as the IRA, "the Red Army Faction," and "the Red Brigades") during the late twentieth century, who targeted civilians as means to achieving perceived political ends. This is not because they are "less unethical," but, on the contrary, because they are *more* unethical, for both consequential (the results of specific actions, calculated in terms of *ex post facto* costs and benefits, usually from a Utilitarian perspective) and deontological (the intrinsic right or wrong of certain actions and our obligation or duty to perform right acts and abstain from wrong ones, usually from a Kantian normative framework) reasons.

From a consequentialist perspective, terror bombings of civilians during wartime have resulted in many *more* casualties (millions of dead and wounded) than *all* acts of "terrorism from below" combined. Furthermore, they have rarely resulted in achieving their declared political objectives: The firebombings of German and Japanese cities did *not* by themselves significantly induce the German and Japanese governments to surrender, rather, they tended to harden to resolve of the indigenous populations to fight harder (as did the German *Blitz* of England during 1940). Even the nuclear bombings of Hiroshima and Nagasaki did not significantly influence, or accelerate, the outcome of the War in the Pacific, because the Japanese government seems willing to have surrendered *before* the bombings. On the other hand, the terror firebombing of Rotterdam in 1940 (which, apparently, may not have been *intended* by the *Luftwaffe*)[14] was followed almost immediately by the surrender of the Dutch to the Germans; and Serbia did withdraw from Kosovo soon after Belgrade and other Yugoslavian cities were bombed by NATO in 1999.[15] But in these two cases, the bombing was brief and civilian casualties were probably in the hundreds, and not in the hundreds of thousands, as they were in Germany and Japan during World War II.

Accordingly, the terror bombings committed by Great Britain and the United States, as well as by Nazi Germany and by Japan (principally in China), are classic examples of "terrorism from above" (TFA) or "state terrorism" (ST) and *they resulted in millions of civilian casualties, without accomplishing their most important political objectives,* namely, the profound demoralization of the civilian populations and prompt surrender of their antagonists. But what these state terrorists *did* accomplish, like their "terrorists from below" counterparts, was the *terrorization* of huge numbers of people, the use of persons as means to alleged political ends, and the dehumanization and denial of dignity to the objects of their terror bombings. And this is unethical by any known moral criterion.

To sum up the commonalities and differences between TFA and TFB in terms of their respective degrees of moral culpability for terrorizing and/or killing many innocent (and possibly a few "guilty") people, while both are unethical, TFA usually *exceeds* TFB in its moral reprehensibility in terms of the:

1. *Magnitude, or scale, of terror*, TFA, or State Terrorism, is immeasurably more pernicious than TFB, since nation-states under Hitler and Stalin killed and/or terrorized tens of millions of their own citizens in the 1930's and 1940s, and slaughtered millions of "enemies" during World War II. Japan, Great Britain, and the United States also killed and/or terrorized millions of "enemies" in Chinese and German cities during that war. Latin American, African, and Asian despots and dictators, many with American support, killed and/or terrorized many thousands of their own citizens during the twentieth century. And the United States has used "precision bombing" and "counterinsurgency" campaigns to kill and/or terrorize millions of Vietnamese and other Southeast Asians, as well as civilians in countries ranging from Afghanistan to Somalia. In comparison, the collective efforts of TFB groups, ranging from the IRA and PFLP to al-Qaeda, have probably resulted in fewer than 10,000 casualties—a tragedy for all the victims and their families, but in scale not comparable to TFA "collateral damage."

2. *The culpability, or degree of legal and/or ethical responsibility*, of the people who made the decisions to terrorize and/or kill people unfortunate enough to be living in states at war with their own is also disproportionately skewed toward TFA. Such decision-makers as Hitler, Stalin, Truman, Churchill, Pol Pot, and L.B. Johnson, who collectively issued orders resulting in the deaths of tens of millions of noncombatants and the terrorization of millions of their compatriots, rarely if ever engaged in personally overseeing the soldiers, sailors, and bombardiers who "were just following" (their) "orders." On the contrary: they were distant and detached from the mass killings that resulted from their policies, and would probably have refused to acknowledge their culpability for any "war crimes" and/or "crimes against humanity"—had they ever been called before an institution such as the International Court of Justice. In contrast, most leaders of TFB subnational groups are themselves directly involved in the terrorist operations, and may even put their lives at risk "for the sake of the cause." They may rationalize what they do, and justify mass murder by appeals to political motives (as do TFA decision-makers), but they would be, and have been, held

individually legally culpable for their "crimes against humanity," unlike virtually all of their TFB counterparts (the international war crimes tribunals being held in The Hague to try Serbian leaders may set a notable precedent for TFA decision-makers to be held legally culpable for crimes against humanity, in this case, for the denial of human rights to and slaughter of Croats and Bosnians).

TFA and TFB *share comparable degrees* moral culpability because:

1. *They instrumentalize and reify the victims of their terrorist tactics.* Both TFA and TFB turn civilian noncombatants and combatants alike into disposable means to be used (or terrorized) in order to achieve perceived political ends. As Susan Sontag (citing Simone Weil), notes "Violence turns anybody subjected to it into a thing."[16]

2. *They dehumanize, objectify, and demonize their real and perceived "enemies,"* including the leaders of other nations or groups ("The Great Satan," "The Evil One," etc.). They also frequently polarize the conflicting parties, esteeming themselves and their followers as "good and virtuous," with "God on our side," and denigrating their opponents as "wicked, evil" and frequently "in-" (or sub-) "human." Citizens of other states who are killed and/or terrorized by their subordinates' tactics are denoted as "collateral damage," and "body counts" of those killed are often employed as quantitative measures of an "operation's" "success."

3. *They use or threaten to use violence on a mass scale*, often disregarding and/or prematurely discarding nonviolent means of conflict resolution. From a crude utilitarian perspective, the "costs" of "inadvertent" and or "unintentional"—but *nevertheless predictable and foreseeable* "friendly fire" and/or "collateral damage" are reflexively seen by many decision-makers to be outweighed by the perceived "benefits" of "victory." Dialogue, negotiation, diplomacy, compromise, the use of nonviolent tactics and/or of nonlethal force, and the recourse to international institutions, are often regarded *by both* TFA and TFB as, at best futile, and at worst weak and defeatist.

4. *Weapons of Mass Destruction* (WMD), *including but not limited to chemical, biological, and nuclear weapons, are desirable "assets"* to both TFA and TFB, even though the use of such weapons on a significant scale may have global—even omnicidal (the death of all humans, including those who give the orders to use the WMD) and therefore suicidal—consequences. WMD Terrorism is the logical extension of the "logic of deterrence" and the "ethics of retaliation" (a version of *lex talionis*).

Consequently, this "Age of Global Terrorism," dating from the early twentieth century, when "total war" and "strategic bombing" became acceptable components of military and diplomatic strategy, has culminated in the progressive obliteration of important previously-held distinctions. *Most notably, there has been a gradual collapse of the distinction between "illegitimate" (i.e. civilian noncombatants) and "legitimate" (i.e. military) "targets," as well as of the distinction between "terrorists" and "the states" (and peoples...) who, allegedly, "support them."*

Finally, this century-long process is leading to the erosion of the boundary between "terrorism" and "war," to such a degree that, since at least the early days of World War II, for the civilian populations of the affected states, war has, ipso facto, become indistinguishable from terrorism. Terrorism, or *psychological* warfare, has become a predictable tool to be employed by war planners and policy-makers. This turn of events is on the one hand a regression to the kind of "barbarism" that preceded the rise of "civilization" about 5,000 years ago in the Ancient Near East, and on the other hand is a seemingly inevitable consequence of technological "progress" *un*accompanied by a comparable "moral evolution" on the parts of the proponents, practitioners, and apologists for TFA and TFA alike.

THE FUTURE OF TERRORISM, AND THE TERRORS OF THE FUTURE

Everyone has the right to life, liberty, and security of person.
Universal Declaration of Human Rights, Article 3, United Nations

Only by the elimination of terrorism's root causes can the world hope to succeed in greatly reducing it if not putting an end to it.[17]

Haig Khatchadourian

World peace will be achieved only by a new politics (and)...rests on two premises: First, on *free will*—right and justice are to rule instead of force. Second, on reality—the human world is not and will never be one of right and perfect justice, but man can strive to make progress on the road to justice.[18]

Karl Jaspers

The cardinal principles of humanitarian law are aimed at the protection of the civilian and civilian objects. States must never make civilians the objects of attack and must consequently never use weapons that are incapable of distinguishing between civilian and military targets.
The International Court of Justice, Paragraph 78, *Legality of the Threat Or Use of Nuclear Weapons*, Advisory Opinion, July, 8 1996

Have compassion with your enemy.
>   Robert S. McNamara, "Lesson" from "The Fog of War"

And how long shall we have to wait before the rest of mankind become pacifists too? There is no telling. But it may not be Utopian to hope that these two factors, the cultural attitude and the justified dread of the consequence of a future war, may result within a measurable time in putting an end to the waging of war. By what paths or by what side-tracks this will come about we cannot guess. But one thing we *can* say: whatever fosters the growth of culture works at the same time against war.[19]
>   Sigmund Freud

Over two millennia ago, the great Roman writer and rhetorician Cicero asked, "What can be done against force, without force?" The answer is "maybe a great deal, maybe very little; it depends on the situation." But to assume that the only, or best, "realistic" response to the use of deadly force, and/or terror, is to reply either "in kind" or with even greater force, is virtually to guarantee that our common future will be even more terrifying than has been our collective history.

Is this the future we wish our descendants to have?

Is there a viable alternative to *realpolitik*, the logic of power underlying the political relations among nations, great and small, and "justifying" the seemingly perpetual cycle of violence committed by decision-makers and their followers ostensibly in the name of "peace, freedom, security, and God's will?"

Are terror and terrorism a portal into our common human condition, which, like the Earth on which it is nested, appears to be contingent, finite, and parlous? What do the existence of terror and terrorism reveal about the world, one in which our worst fears may indeed come true? Is the future of terrorism to include an ever-escalating series of attacks and counterattacks culminating in global annihilation? Or can such hypothetical, but foreseeable, terrors be minimized by the judicious application of self-restraint and self-control on the one hand, and by nonviolent means of conflict avoidance and resolution on the other hand?

If terror continues to be used to fight terrorism, it is much more likely that terror will increase, not decrease, and that terrorism will spread, not contract, perhaps indefinitely. *There can be no end to terror, because terror seems rooted in our psycho-physiological constitution, in our condition. Therefore, to end terror would mean to end humanity, or at least the human condition as we now know it. It would entail the reconstitution of our mental, neurobiological, and existential condition— the radical transformation of our brains, and the redirection of our history.* This is conceivable but highly unlikely, at least in the foreseeable future.

On the other hand, there can be an diminution, if not an end, to terrorism, if nations, decision-makers, and warriors on all sides, of every political and religious persuasion, can learn that the terror spawned by all forms of terrorism is not only deeply unethical, but is also usually ineffective in promoting the political and other ends supposedly served by the murderous armamentarium of terrorism.

The Human Story: A Comedy of Errors or an Epic Tragedy?

We are entering a period of human history that may provide an answer to the question of whether it is better to be smart [like humans] or stupid [like beetles and bacteria]. The most hopeful prospect is that the question will *not* be answered: if it receives a definitive answer, that answer can only be that humans were a kind of "biological error," using their allotted 100,000 years [the average life expectancy of a species on Earth] to destroy themselves and, in the process, much else.[20]

Noam Chomsky

By painful experience we have learned that rational thinking does not suffice to solve the problems of our social life. Penetrating research and keen scientific work have often had tragic implications for mankind, producing, on the one hand, inventions which liberated man from exhausting physical labor, making his life easier and richer; but on the other hand introducing a grave restlessness into his life making him a slave to his technological environment, and—most catastrophic of all—creating the means for his own destruction. This is indeed a tragedy of overwhelming poignancy![21]

Albert Einstein

The contingency of the future, which accounts for the violent acts of those in power, by the same token deprives these acts of all legitimacy, or equally legitimates the violence of their opponents. The right of the opposition is exactly equal to the right of those in power.... a problem which has troubled Europe since the Greeks, namely, *that the human condition may be such that it has no happy solution....* Does not every action involve us in a game we cannot entirely control? Is there not a sort of evil in collective life? At least in times of crisis, does not each freedom encroach upon the freedom of other?... Is not our choice always good and always bad?[22]

Maurice Merleau-Ponty

People like myself want not a world in which murder no longer exists (we are not as crazy as that!) but rather one in which murder is not legitimate. Here indeed we are Utopian—and contradictory. *For we do live, it is true, in a world where murder is legitimate, and we ought to change it if we do not like it. But it appears that we cannot change it without risking murder. Murder thus throws us back on murder, and we will continue to live in terror whether we accept the fact with resignation or wish to abolish it by means which merely replace one terror with another....* For what strikes me...is the fundamental good will of every one. From Right to Left, every one, with the exception for a few swindlers, believes that his particular truth is the one to make men happy. And yet the combination of all these good intentions has produced the present infernal world, where men are killed, threatened and deported, where war is prepared, where one cannot speak freely without being insulted or betrayed....All I ask is that, in the midst of a murderous world, we agree to reflect on murder and to make a choice. After that, we can distinguish those who accept the consequences of being murderers themselves or the accomplices of murderers, and those who refuse to do so with all of their being....And henceforth, the only honorable course will be to stake everything on a formidable gamble: that words are more powerful than munitions.[23]

Albert Camus

In the fourth century before Christ, Western antiquity's greatest philosopher-scientist, Aristotle, created the first known systematic treatise on poetry and drama, the *Poetics*. In that work, Aristotle delineated a view of tragedy that still dominates most discussions of this quintessentially humanistic art form.

To Aristotle, "tragedy...is an imitation not only of a complete action but also of incidents arousing pity and fear."[24] (We may safely translate "pity and fear"—*pathos* and *phobos*—as compassion and terror....) Aristotle was essentially concerned with depicting tragedy as a structured (beginning, middle, and end) plot whose aim and purpose is to "imitate" the rise of fall of good but often fatally flawed *individuals*, such as the kings and "tyrants" of the ancient world—whose demise is often occasioned by their own actions, witting or unwitting. In modern (and postmodern?) times, however, we are confronted with a more encompassing kind of tragedy—a compassion and terror-arousing narrative of the suffering victims and perpetrators of terror (such as the 52 terror victims I interviewed, each of whom is individually "tragic" in his or her own way...) who are *also* players in the "epic" rise and fall of nations, empires, superpowers, and perhaps of the human species itself.[25]

If the history of terrorism and the psychology of terror have anything to teach us about the tragic dimension of our human condition, it is that virtually all of us are prone to "losing it," to going wildly "out of control" when wracked with tormenting anxieties and internal fantasies or when attacked by external "enemies" we perceive to be mortal threats to our selves and our existence. One of the most prominent "roots of evil," is "threatened egotism," and what often follows from wounded narcissism is rage that culminates in violent revenge.[26]

Rage—unreasoning and "natural"—is an all-too-human response to real and perceived threats to our lives, liberty, property, and security. Intense anger is often the mirror and expression of intense fear. But this is an impulse that must be controlled, especially by political and military decision-makers, who must learn not to avenge tragic attacks on the polity and its people, but to restrain their natural inclination to "match fire with fire" and instead to seek multilateral diplomatic and legal ways to address heinous crimes against humanity. For what will ultimately determine the fate of our species, and the preservation or termination of our condition, is *not which causes we pursue*—such as freedom and democracy, or jihad and the will of God—*but the means we use to defend and advance them.*

Violence and nonviolence are not absolutes, and neither are war and peace. *There is a broad spectrum of actions (and even thoughts...) involving the use of force*, ranging from slaps across the face and gentle admonitions on the *less* violent end of the spectrum, to the detonation of WMD and the deployment of missives of mass deception on the ultraviolent and malevolent end of the spectrum. Absolute pacifism, or complete nonviolence, is a lofty ideal, but is rarely if ever practicable. *On the other hand, the use (and even the threatened use...) of modern weaponry, whether "justified" by "reasons of state and national security," or "sanctified" by "divine" authority, may lead to mass murder on an unprecedented scale—as well as to potential extermination* (and this is following a century in which over 100 million people, mostly civilians, died during wars and genocidal mass murder committed by decision-makers against their own and/or foreign populations).

What is desperately needed is a political strategy that protects the rights and personhood of as many people as possible, while diminishing if not extinguishing the global existential threat posed by terrorism in all its guises. The components of such a strategy have long been available, and they include the vast range of nonviolent tactics and actions practiced by such peaceful warriors as Gandhi and Martin Luther King, promulgated as potentially efficacious means of civilian defense by Gene Sharp, and proposed as *nonlethal* "weapons" to deter and subdue, but not destroy, those who would cause mayhem.[27] While it is easy to be seduced into reflexively believing that our options are restricted to "a war against terrorism" or "appeasement," in fact this is a "Hobson's choice," and a false dilemma, since it excludes more conciliatory, multidimensional approaches to such enormously difficult, and possibly intractable, political/psychological problems as terrorism.

A "mix" of nonviolent law-enforcement, diplomatic, and economic measures, combined with forceful but nonlethal tactics, may or may not succeed in lessoning terrorist attacks.[28] In those few cases where nonviolent and nonlethal strategies have been tried but have failed to deter or eliminate real terrorist threats, strictly pinpointed attacks on individual "terrorist cells"—both "from above and from below"—by small, mobile, highly trained "rapid deployment forces," preferably under UN supervision, could be attempted to apprehend and if possible arrest terrorism suspects. If the alleged terrorists resist violently, then, of course, self-defense by rapid deployment forces would be appropriate, even if it led to unintended deaths and injuries among the suspected terrorists. But it is difficult to imagine a scenario when strategic or tactical bombing, especially of cities and villages, could be justified. Still, one never knows in advance what the unintended consequences of one's actions may be. And while mistakes are inevitable, the chance of "unintentionally" doing violence to noncombatants is minimized if not eliminated if weapons that might engender "collateral damage" are rarely if ever used.

History suggests that state terrorism from above usually fails to achieve its political aims and often results in the deaths of innocents and the violent revenge of their kith and kin. The Romans eventually lost to the "barbarians"; the French and the United States were forced to exit Vietnam; the Russians withdrew from Afghanistan, and despite two "wars" they have not subdued Chechen insurgents, and so on. But revolutionary/insurrectionary terrorism from below also has an unpromising historical legacy. For example, the Chechen insurgents, despite a terrorist campaign carried to the heart of Moscow, have not gained their independence from Russia, and ETA has not managed to force or coax the Spanish government to grant independence to the Basque country (possible counterexamples to the historical tendency for terrorism from below to fail may be the Algerian war for independence from France and the Bolshevik-led revolution in Russia). *The point is that political violence, whether from above or from below, does not by itself wipe out insurgencies, overthrow just or unjust governments, or achieve independence for separatist movements. Only viable political programs accompanied by widespread and largely nonviolent social movements can accomplish those aims.*

Similarly, a "war against terrorism"—"the plague of the 21st century," in the words of Russian President Vladimir Putin—or a "jihad against Anglo-American hegemony," is unlikely to be "won" or "lost" by force of arms alone. Putin's "formula" for conducting such a "war," or counterinsurgency campaign, against Chechens—"Russia does not negotiate with terrorists. Russia eliminates them"[29]—is similar to Ariel Sharon's murderous tactics to quell Palestinian resistance to Israeli occupation and to stop terrorist attacks against Israelis. Both efforts are unlikely to be successful because the grassroots support for Chechen and Palestinian political goals is likely to be increased, not diminished, by terrorism from above perpetrated by Russian and Israeli armed forces. The assassinations of indigenous political leaders—who may or may not be "terrorists" but whose human and legal rights must be safeguarded—is usually accompanied by the killings of innocent bystanders. This is also true for jihadists and "freedom fighters" with real and perceived grievances against such powerful states as Russia, Israel, and the United States. A "war against imperialism" is just as ethically and politically dubious as "the war against terrorism." For in both cases, might does not make right, and the murdered and maimed victims of these wars have families and friends who will seek to avenge their deaths, thus perpetuating a cycle of violence and terrorism, and leading to war unending.

Military interventions, if used at all, must be few, far between, and serve only to accompany a comprehensive diplomatic, legal, and socioeconomic plan to identify, address, and remediate the long-standing roots of and reasons for terrorist activities of all kinds, from above and below. Such a strategy would include a fair and practicable peace and social justice plan for the Near and Far East, including but not limited to the end of Israel's occupation of Palestine and the creation of a viable Palestinian state; the phased withdrawal of American and coalition armed forces from Iraq, Saudi Arabia, Kuwait, the Gulf States and Afghanistan and their replacement by UN-sponsored peacekeepers and support personnel; the implementation of a multilateral plan for a negotiated settlement for the uses of nuclear and other energy sources by Iran and North Korea, as well as security guarantees in exchange for the cessation of WMD programs; the gradual implementation of nuclear/WMD-free zones, most immediately in the Near East, South Asia, and the Far East; and the phased disarmament of all weapons of mass and vast destruction globally—most importantly (but reluctantly) by the current nuclear states. Enraged and terrified politicians, soldiers, civilians, and freedom-fighters cannot blow their "enemies"—and themselves—to pieces if they do not have the weapons to do so.

An open-ended "war on terror" may, ironically and tragically, bring about the very phenomena it is allegedly designed to deter and defeat: the proliferation of weapons of mass and vast destruction; the spread of terrorism and terrorist cells to nations previously without them; the loss of thousands, perhaps millions, of civilians and soldiers; and the actual use of biological, chemical, and/or nuclear weapons, both locally and globally, leading to the apocalyptic violence the war on terror(ism) was supposed to prevent. The "lesser evil," also ironically, is classical terrorism from below, since, at present, it does not appear to have the resources to "defeat" the "greater evil," terrorism from above.

Terrorism from below can probably wipe out cities, perhaps even small nations. Terrorism from above—nuclear state terrorism—can annihilate the human race and possibly end all life on Earth. This confrontation could figuratively and literally lead to Armageddon, since the two nuclear states considered by many Europeans and most Arabs to be the greatest threats to world peace and global security—the United States and Israel—not only are the major targets of Islamist terrorism, but are also the countries (along with Pakistan and India) most prone to use their weapons of mass and/or vast destruction in pursuit of their strategic political goals.[30]

The ultimate, and last, "clash of civilizations," to use Samuel P. Huntington's infelicitous but possibly prophetic term, could well occur within shooting distance of where Western civilization arose, the Middle East. And Armageddon, in the biblical and fundamentalist Christian senses of the term, may well be a self-fulfilling prophecy—so long as fundamentalists of all religious and political creeds believe absolutely in the "rightness" of their cause, the "evil" of their adversaries, and the "legitimacy" of using any means necessary to "defeat the evil One." The road to Armageddon is paved with patriotic, parochial, and "peace-loving" intentions.

We, as a species, as custodians of terrestrial life, can either take immediate action—with as little violence as possible and as much coercion as necessary—to stop and reverse the vicious cycle of terror from above, terrorism from below, and murderous violence from above and below. We might, or might not, thereby slow and halt an increasingly terrifying planet-wide confrontation. Or we stand by and risk being consumed by a conflagration that could potentially incinerate this small emerald planet.

The ironic denouement of the epic tragedy of human history might well be that there would be no playwrights remaining to depict our fall from dominion over Earth, and the return of planetary rule to the microbes and cockroaches that preceded us. We, the lords of earthly creation, would have passed from the worldly stage we have constructed and demolished. Our fear and terror of personal and social disintegration would have engendered the rage and terrorism leading to global annihilation. And like the inaudible scream of existential terror, so glaringly and garishly colored by Edvard Munch, the voice of humanity would have vanished from the cosmos, unheard and ineffable. The choice of action—the beginning of the end of all forms of terrorism, or the end of humankind—is ours.

NOTES

1 DEFINING THE INDEFINABLE: WHAT ARE AND ARE NOT "TERROR, TERRORISM, AND THE HUMAN CONDITION?"

1. For two very different but perceptive and sometimes alarming accounts of what "really" happened on September 11, 2001, and why it was not prevented, see *Inside 9–11 What Really Happened*, by the Reporters, Writers, and Editors of *Der Spiegel* Magazine (New York: St. Martin's Press, 2002); and Gerald Posner, *Why America Slept The Failure to Prevent 9/11* (New York: Random House, 2003).
2. Mark A. Schuster et al., "A National Survey of Stress Reactions after the September 11, 2001, Terrorist Attacks," *New England Journal of Medicine*, 345:20 (November 15, 2001), 1,507–12. Also see Susan Coates, Jane Rosenthal, and Daniel Schechter, *September 11 Trauma and Human Bonds* (Hillsdale, NJ, and London: The Analytic Press, 2003).
3. Sandro Galea et al., "Psychological Sequelae of the September 11 Terrorist Attacks in New York City," *New England Journal of Medicine*, 346:13 (March 28, 2002), 982–87.
4. Alexander N. Ortega and Robert Rosenheck, "Posttraumatic Stress Disorder among Hispanic Vietnam Veterans," *American Journal of Psychiatry*, 157:4 (April 2000), 615–19.
5. William E. Schlenger et al., "Psychological Reactions to Terrorist Attacks: Findings from the National Study of Americans' Reactions to September 11," *Journal of the American Medical Association*, 288 (2002), 581–88.
6. Roxane C. Silver, et al., "Nationwide Longitudinal Study of Psychological Responses to September 11," *Journal of the American Medical Association*, 288 (2002), 1,235–44.
7. DCI Counterterrorist Center, Central Intelligence Agency (undated), 3.
8. Haig Khatchadourian, *The Morality of Terrorism* (New York: Peter Lang Publishing, 1998), 11.
9. Bruce Hoffman, "Lessons of 9/11" (Santa Monica, CA, RAND, CT-201, October 2002).
10. Igor Primoratz, "What is Terrorism?" *Journal of Applied Philosophy*, 7:2, (1990), 129–30.

11. Richard Falk has argued that "'Terrorism' as a word and concept became associated in US and Israeli political discourse with *anti*-state forms of violence that were so criminal that any method of enforcement and retaliation was viewed as acceptable, and not subject to criticism. By so appropriating the meaning of this inflammatory term in such a self-serving manner, terrorism became detached from its primary historical association dating back to the French Revolution. In that formative setting, *the state's own political violence against its citizens*, violence calculated to induce widespread fear and achieve political goals, was labeled as terrorism, most famously by Edmund Burke. ... With the help of the influential media, the state over time has waged and largely won the battle of definitions by exempting its own violence against civilians from being treated and perceived as 'terrorism.' Instead such violence was generally discussed as 'uses of force,' 'retaliation,' 'self-defense,' and 'security measures.'" Not to mention "preemptive wars," "counterinsurgency," and "counterterrorism." Richard Falk, *The Great Terror War* (New York: Olive Branch Press, 2003), xviii–xix.

12. Khatchadourian, *The Morality of Terrorism*, 4–11; Bruce Hoffman, *Inside Terrorism* (New York: Columbia University Press, 1998), 13–43; and Johan Galtung, Carl G. Jacobsen, and Kai Frithjof Brand-Jacobsen, *Searching for Peace The Road to Transcend* (London and Sterling, Virginia: Pluto Press, 2002), 87–89. Khatchadourian, following Paul Wilkinson, is one of the very few scholars to mention the *psychological* component of terrorism, viz., *terror*, but he also claims that "although 'terror' can exist in the absence of terrorism, Wilkinson wrongly thinks that political terrorism always involves 'terror..,' wrongly because unlike 'terror..,' political terrorism is almost invariable a sustained policy." But there are many counterexamples of political terrorism, especially from below, that, especially in the cases of assassinations (of presidents, czars, prime ministers, and other state officials), are singular and/or episodic. Khatchadourian concedes, however, that "admittedly, it" (political terrorism) "shares some of the characteristics of 'terror.' It is ruthlessly destructive, unpredictable, and frequently indiscriminate with respect to its immediate victims, although not its real target, the victimized" (9). Hoffman also mentions the "far-reaching psychological effects"—namely fear and intimidation—of terrorist attacks (44) but his main focus, as with virtually all analysts of terrorism, is elsewhere.

13. See Khatchadourian, ibid., 6–7. A clear of example of (potential) "criminal" terrorism would be if the alleged terrorist group AZF did in fact detonate a bomb in the French railway system if it is not paid the money it is apparently demanding from the French government (see "Terrorist Bomb Threats Endanger French Railways," Elaine Sciolino, *The New York Times*, March 4, 2004, A3). Cases of blackmail and extortion may involve terrorist threats to civilians, but they are not *political* terrorism unless there is a predominantly *political* component in their strategy.

14. See Jürgen Habermas in Giovanna Borradori, *Philosophy in a Time of Terror: Dialogues with Jürgen Habermas and Jacques Derrida* (Chicago and London: The University of Chicago Press, 2003), xii–xiii and 25–43. According to Noam Chomsky, "Terrorism is the use of coercive means aimed at civilian populations to achieve political, religious, or other aims. That's what the World Trade Center attack was, a particularly horrifying terrorist crime. Terrorism, according to the official definitions, is simply part of state action, official doctrine, and not just of the U.S., of course." And, "alongside the literal meaning of the term.., there is also a propagandistic usage ..: the term 'terrorism' is used to refer to terrorist acts committed by enemies against us or our allies. ... Even the Nazis harshly condemned terrorism and carried out what they called 'counter-terrorism' against the terrorist partisans." 9/11 (New York: Seven Stories Press, 2001), 57 and 90. In a subsequent book, *Hegemony or Survival America's Quest for Global Dominance* (New York: Metropolitan Books, 2003), 110, Chomsky claims that "a convenient definition of terrorism was adopted" by the Bush (II) administration, namely "terrorism is what our leaders declare it to be. Period." Later in that book, Chomsky partly concurs with former American Secretary of State George Shultz, that "terrorism is indeed an intolerable return to barbarism," but "perceptions about its nature differ sharply at opposite ends of the guns" (208–09). Also see the insightful online article "Defining Terrorism" by Michael Kinsley (Washington post.com/ wp–dyn/articles/A8709-2001Oct4.html), who lists the political advantages of the Bush administration framing its "mission as a 'war against terrorism,' not just against the perpetrators of the particular crime of Sept. 11" (1) and argues that "the concept of terrorism is supposed to be a shortcut to the moral high ground. That is what makes it so useful. It says: The end doesn't justify the means. We don't need to argue about whose cause is right and whose is wrong, because certain behavior makes you the bad guy however noble your cause." This political construction of "terrorism and terrorists" (as was the "Cold War" against "international Communism" and "Communist subversion" in the United States and abroad) is used to justify virtually anything, especially the use of war and "counterterrorism," as a "moral" imperative; in fact, it is more propaganda than ethics.

15. *Webster's Third New International Dictionary* defines terror as "a state of intense fright or apprehension: stark fear," as well as "one that inspires fear: threat, scourge"; and "reign of terror" (Ibid., 2,361). A "terrorist," according to this dictionary, is "an advocate or practitioner of terror as a means of coercion; especially Jacobin," and "one who panics or causes anxiety: alarmist" (Ibid., 2,361). And "terrorism" is "the systematic use of terror as a means of coercion," and "an atmosphere of threat and violence" (Ibid., 2,361). Note the *explicitly psychological, political, and historical* dimensions of terror, terrorist, and terrorism, as well as the *absence* of a specification regarding the perpetrators (no

"state/non-state" differentiation) and victims (no distinction between "civilians"/"combatants").

16. Two other approaches should also be noted. One is evident in an American anthropology text called *Cultural Anthropology A Perspective on the Human Condition*, fifth Edition, by Emily Schulz and Robert Lavenda (Mountain View: Mayfield Publishing Company, 2001). The authors declare that "the human condition is distinguished from the conditions of other living species by culture" (Ibid., 18), and that "culture (which)...is learned, shared, adaptive, and symbolic ...has ...evolved, over millions of years" (Ibid., 19). Further, "the human condition is rooted in time and shaped by history. ...Hence, human history is an essential aspect of the human story" (Ibid. 27). A related approach is exemplified by the work of the noted psychiatrist/anthropologist Arthur Kleinman, who, in *The Illness Narratives Suffering, Healing, and the Human Condition* (New York: Basic Books, 1988), following the German phenomenologist Helmut Plessner, depicts the "divided nature of the human condition in the West: namely, that each of us *is* his/her body and *has* (experiences) a body....As a result, the sick both are their illnesses and are distanced, even alienated, from the illness" (26). While it is noticeable that these authors do *not* go on to examine the notion of "the human condition" in any detail, their approaches for studying it are important. I return to the cultural, historical, phenomenological, and somatic aspects of terror, terrorism, and the human condition in subsequent chapters.

17. Hannah Arendt, *The Human Condition* (Garden City: Doubleday Anchor Books, 1959), 2.

18. Ibid., 10–11.

19. Ibid., 19.

20. Albert Camus, *The Rebel* (New York: Vintage Books, 1956), 101.

21. Albert Camus, *The Myth of Sisyphus* (New York: Vintage Books, 1955), 86.

22. Paul Tillich, *The Courage to Be* (New Haven: Yale University Press, 1971), 38.

23. Ibid., 64.

24. Thomas Keating, *The Human Condition* (New York: Paulist Press, 1999), 10.

25. Arendt, *The Human Condition*, 3.

2   Depiciting the undesirable: A Brief History of Terrorism

(For this part of the book, I am deeply indebted to Charles Lindholm, University Professor at Boston University, who wrote much of the section in this chapter on the Middle East.)

1. Bruce Hoffman, "Lessons of 9/11" (RAND, CT-201, October 2002).

2. Walter Laqueur, *The Age of Terrorism* (Boston: Little Brown & Company, 1987), 3,9, and 143.

3. Caleb Carr, *The Lessons of Terror* (New York: Random House, 2002), 12–13.

4. In some places I use inverted commas to denote "terrorism" and/or "terrorists," but not in other places. This is intentional, but it may jar some readers—especially those who believe that these terms are self-explanatory. Unfortunately, they are not. They are two of the most hotly contested terms in the political lexicon. And there is no universally-agreed-upon rule to designate the "proper" usage of these words. Nonetheless, in this book, quotation marks will appear around "terrorism" and "terrorist" when the context in which theses terms are used decrees that the term may still be *widely contested* (as in a history of terrorism, during which time many alleged "terrorist" incidents were committed by "terrorists" who have been deemed by at least some authorities as "freedom fighters," political "heroes," "*jihadists,*" etc.). At other times, terrorism and terrorists appear without quotation marks. In these cases, the terms seem *significantly less contested* (as in the terrorist attacks of September 11, 2001, as well as the assassinations/murders and bombings perpetrated by ETA in Spain—although even here there are some claim that those responsible for these attacks are "*jihadists*" fighting a "holy war" against "infidels," on the one hand, or nationalists, resistance-fighters, and/or "anti-imperialists," on the other hand—but not "terrorists"). Readers are of course free to make their own determinations as to whether or not a specific attack was "terrorist" or not, and if those who perpetrated the attack were or were not "terrorists." The terrifying *effects*, however, of those acts of violence, are the common denominator of all these attacks. And, therefore, *terror, not terrorism,* is the central focus of this book.

5. See Carr, Laqueur, and Hoffman, *Inside Terrorism,* as well as Paul Wilkinson, *Political Terrorism* (Hoboken: John Wiley & Sons, 1974), and Peter Waldmann, *Terrorismus Provokation der Macht* (Munich: Gerling Akadamie Verlag, 1998), esp. 40–55.

6. Jean Bethke Elshtain, *Just War against Terror* (New York: Basic Books, 2003), 50.

7. Aristotle, *Politics* (13,142), cited in Michael Walzer, *Just and Unjust Wars* (New York: Basic Books, 1977), 198.

8. See David Barash and Charles Webel, *Peace and Conflict Studies* (Thousand Oaks, London, and New Delhi: Sage Publications, 2002), 4–5.

9. Ibid., 146–47.

10. See Laqueur, *The Age of Terrorism,* 12–13; Hoffman, *Inside Terrorism,* 88–89; Karen Armstrong, *Holy War* (New York: Random House, 2001), 18–19; and Jessica Stern, *Terror in the Name of God* (New York: Harper/Collins Ecco, 2003), xxi-xxii, for conventional histories of this period.

11. See Carr, *The Lessons of Terror,* chapter 1, for a good account of the brutal, terror-inducing, and often futile measures deployed by the Romans against those who rebelled (especially the Carthaginians and German tribes) against their dominion. Many books (and films, including the spectacularly commercially successful if historically imperfect

Academy Award–winning epic *Gladiator*) detail the violence used internally and abroad by Roman leaders (beginning with Julius Caesar's own account of *The Gallic Wars)* and emperors.

12. Mohmmad, al-Ghazali, *The Foundation of the Articles of Faith,* trans. Nahi Amin Faris (Lahore: Ashraf Press, 1963), 134 .

13. Ignaz Goldziher, *Introduction to Islamic Law and Theology* (Princeton: Princeton University Press, 1981), 183.

14. Patricia Crone and Martin Hinds, *God's Caliph: Religious Authority in the First Centuries of Islam* (Cambridge: Cambridge University Press, 1986), 130 and 132.

15. M.W. Watt, *The Formative Period of Islamic Thought* (Edinburgh: Edinburgh University Press, 1973), 20.

16. See Gilles Kepel, *Jihad The Trail of Political Islam* (Cambridge: Harvard University Press 2002), 24–30, for the Muslim Brotherhood; John L. Esposito, *Unholy War Terror in the Name of Islam* (Oxford: Oxford University Press, 2002), 84–87, for Islamic Jihad and Jamaat-i-Islami; and Ahmed Rashid, *Taliban* (New Haven: Yale University Press, 2000). Also see Jessica Stern, *Terror in the Name of God,* for interviews with many contemporary Islamic "terrorists."

17. For a synopsis of the differences between Sunni and Shi'ite Muslims, see Bernard Lewis, *The Middle East* (New York: Simon and Schuster Touchstone Books, 1997), 67 and 139.

18. M.A. Shaban, *Islamic History, A New Interpretation: A.D. 600–750 A.H. 132* (Cambridge: Cambridge University Press, 1971), 183.

19. For the Seljuk Empire and the Isamaili Shi'ites, see Karen Armstrong, *Islam* (New York: The Modern Library, 2000), 85–89.

20. See Laqueur, *The Age of Terrorism*, 13, for a description of the Assassins.

21. See Chalmers Johnson, *Blowback* (New York: Henry Holt, 2000), 8, for a searing account of "blowback," a term, which, according to Johnson, "officials of the Central Intelligence Agency first invented for their own internal use. … It refers to the unintended consequences of policies that were kept secret from the American public." Some examples are "the malign acts of 'terrorists' or 'drug lords' or 'rogue states' or 'illegal arms merchants,'" who, according to Johnson, "often turn out to be blowback from earlier American operations …. What U.S. officials denounce as unprovoked terrorist attacks on its innocent citizens are often meant as retaliation for previous American imperial actions. Terrorists attack innocent and undefended American targets precisely because American soldiers and sailors firing cruise missiles from ships at sea or sitting in B-52 bombers at extremely high altitudes or supporting brutal and repressive regimes from Washington seem invulnerable . … In addition, the military asymmetry that denies nation states the ability to engage in overt attack against the United States drives the use of transnational actors (that is, terrorists from one country attacking in another)." Ibid., 9.

22. Marshall Hodgeson, *The Order of Assassins: The Struggle of the Early Nizari Ismai'lis Against the Islamic* World ('s-Gravenhage: Mouton, 1955), 81.

23. *Ibid.*, 81.

24. For *Al*-Qaeda's selective appropriation of Western technology and modernity, see John Gray, *Al Qaeda and What It Means to be Modern* (New York: The New Press, 2003).

25. For the importance and impact of Khomeini's revolution, see Kepel, *Jihad The Trail of Political Islam*, 106–35; and Armstrong, *Islam*, 173–75.

26. I have interviewed one of the Americans who in 1979 was kidnapped from the U.S. Embassy in Teheran by followers of Khomeini. His experience, along with the stories of many other contemporary victims of TFB and TFA, will be related in subsequent chapters of this book.

27. Said Amir Arjomand, *The Turban and the Crown: The Islamic Revolution in Iran* (New York: Oxford University Press, 1988).

28. Ayatollah Khomeini, quoted in Yann Richard, *Shi'ite Islam: Polity, Ideology and Creed* (Oxford: Basil Blackwell, 1995), 86.

29. A public opinion poll ("Eurobarometer") conducted of more than 7,500 citizens from 15 states of the European Union indicates that the current Israeli government (closely followed by the Bush administration and the government of North Korea) is considered by many Europeans to be the greatest threat to world peace. See *Yahoo! News*, Mideast-AFP, November 3, 2003.

30. Although there is a popular (mis)conception in most of the West that most suicidal terrorists are Muslim (called "witnesses," or "*shahids*" in Arabic), and that virtually all of them have predominantly *religious* motivations (martyrdom allegedly for the sake of Islam), the facts are that suicide terrorism was historically launched by Jewish Zealots against the Romans centuries before Islam, and that recently the most frequent users of suicide attacks *have been Hindus*—the Tamil Tigers in Sri Lanka. Furthermore, during the nineteenth and twentieth centuries, Christian, Sikh, Buddhist, and Shinto terrorists have also carried out suicide attacks—sometime with, sometimes without, explicitly religious motivations. In addition, Islamist suicide bombers display a *range of secular and/or religious motivations* for their deadly attacks, primarily to take revenge against Israeli raids and "targeted assassinations" and/or to end the Israeli occupation of Palestinian territory. See Andrew Silke, "The Psychology of Suicidal Terrorism," in Andrew Silke, ed., *Terrorists, Victims and Society Psychological Perspectives on Terrorism and Its Consequences* (Chichester, England: John Wiley & Sone, 2003), 93–107.

31. See Kepel, *Jihad The Trail of Political Islam*, 83–85.

32. See Michael Youssef, *Revolt Against Modernity: Muslim Zealots and the West* (Leiden: E.J. Brill, 1985).

33. See Kepel, *Jihad The Trail of Political Islam*, 27–30, and R.P. Mitchell, *The Society of the Muslim Brothers* (Oxford: Oxford University Press, 1969), for Hassan al-Banna and the Muslim Brotherhood.

34. Muhammad Guessous, quoted in Kevin Dwyer, *Arab Voices: The Human Rights Debate in the Middle* East (Berkeley: University of California Press, 1991), 120.

35 . Laqueur, in *The Age of Terrorism*, 8, citing U.S. State Department statistics, claims that from 1980 to 1985 there were many times more acts of terrorism (which Laqueur restricts to acts of violent by *non*-state actors) in Latin America (369) and Western Europe (458) than in the Middle East (84). Since 1985, it is not rash to conclude that this statistical picture has changed dramatically, even if one excludes acts of terrorism from above, which I would not do.

36. Edward S. Herman, *The Real Terror Network Terrorism in Fact and Propaganda* (Boston: South End Press, 1982) 21–22.

37. Laqueur, *The Age of Terrorism,* 146. Laqueur then goes on to state: "A good case, no doubt, can be made in favor of the proposition that too little attention has been paid to state terrorism by historians, sociologists, and political scientists, and too much to individual terrorism. But the case of *obliterating* the basic differences between a regime of terror exercised by the a state and terrorist activities by 'non-state actors' is a very weak one indeed. Both kinds aim at inducing a state of fear among the 'enemy.' But beyond this there are no important similarities" (ibid.). But the deliberate inducement of a "state of fear," aka *terror,* is precisely the point of all perpetrators of terrorism, whether from above (state) or from below (non-state actors).

38. Edward S. Herman and Gerry O'Sullivan compiled a table listing "Killings by state and non-state terrorists: numbers and orders of magnitude," confining themselves to nations (mainly in Latin America and Southeast Asia) and "terrorist groups" (European, PLO, and all "international terrorists," according to the CIA), whose results strikingly confirm Laqueur's claim that during the late twentieth century states (even if one excludes Nazi Germany, Stalin's Soviet Union, Pol Pot's Cambodia, etc., which I would not do) are responsible for hundreds, if not thousands, of times more killings than non-state terrorists. Herman and O'Sullivan, "'Terrorism' as Ideology and Culture Industry," in *Western State Terrorism*, ed. Alexander George (Cambridge: Polity Press, 1992), 41–42. They go on to demonstrate the ways in which Western government sectors and mass media have fabricated an image of "terrorism" and "terrorists" that is far from reality, and that is an essential component of the "terrorism industry" of policy-makers, media moguls, and "terrorism experts."

39. Johan Galtung, "11 September 2001: Diagnosis, Prognosis, Therapy," in Johan Galtung, Carl G. Jacobsen, and Kai Frithjof Brand-Jacobsen *Searching For Peace The Road to Transcend* (London: Pluto Press, 2002),

91–94; William Blum, *Rogue State: A Guide to the World's Only Superpower* (Monroe, MA: Common Courage Press, 2000).

40. It may unnerve, even anger, some readers to read about the "state terrorism" and "rogue" behavior of such two ostensibly democratic and freedom-loving nations as the United States and Israel. Yet the historical record since the last days of World War II cannot be ignored—particularly in terms of the number of civilian victims of American and Israeli military operations and the defiance by the United States and Israel of human rights and international consensus in the world's most democratic public forum, the United Nations. For Israel's use of terrorist methods ("sacred terrorism," according to Edward Herman), initially against the British and then against the Palestinians and Israel's Arab neighbors, as well as for the Palestinians' violent responses, see Carr, *The Lessons of Terror*, 210–21; and Herman, *The Real Terror Network*, 76–79. For numerous examples of the U.S. support of repressive governments and terrorism around the world, and opposition to the United Nations and other "multilateral" organizations and international treaties/norms, see Blum, *Rogue State A Guide to the World's Only Superpower*, esp. 184–99; and Noam Chomsky, *Rogue States The Rule of Force in World Affairs* (Cambridge MA: South End Press, 2000).

41. Ted Honderich, *After the Terror* (Edinburgh: Edinburgh University Press, 2002), 151. Honderich's book has caused an enormous stir in philosophical and other intellectual circles. His argument is regarded by many as an apologia for terrorism, and of blaming the "victims" of terrorism (Westerners) for their own misfortunes. "We need to change the world of bad lives and not just to make more terrorism against us less likely. ... Our societies as they are, if you will put up with some last plain speaking, are ignorant, stupid, selfish, managed and deceived for gain, self-deceived, and deadly" (147). While controversial and at times overstated, Honderich's book is essential reading for anyone interested in the knotty ethical issues intertwined with the political debate on "terrorism" and how to respond to it.

42. Interview by Jessica Stern with a member of the Pakistani group Harkatul-Mujahideen (HUM), an offshoot of Osama bin Laden's International Islamic Front for Jihad against the Jews and Crusaders, in Stern, *Terror in the Name of God Why Religious Militants Kill*, 125–26.

43. James Bennet, "Palestinian Bomber Kills 8 and Wounds 50 in Jerusalem," *The New York Times*, February 23, 2004, A3.

44. In fact, *sura* ("lesson") 17 of the *Qur'an* ("scriptural teachings") states: "Do not kill, save where it is justified, any soul that Allah has made inviolate. We have given authority to the next-of-kin of anyone who is wrongfully killed, but let him not be excessive in the killing, for he himself has been aided." *The Koran, Selected Suras*, translated from the Arabic by Arthur Jeffrey (Mineola, New York: Dover Publications, 2001), 116. Of course, there is considerable debate within and outside

Islam over the meanings of "wrongfully" killed and "excessive" in the killing. But that is also true of all religions and most ethical codes. Terrorism, both from above and from below, would surely be deemed "excessive" and "wrongful" by most devout Muslims, as well as by true believers of all the world's other great religions.

45. For the historical and etymological origins of "terrorism, terrorist, and terror," see Walter Laqueur's account of the French "systeme, regime de la terreur" from 1793 to 1798, and of the hostile British reaction to what Edmund Burke deemed these criminal "hell hounds called 'terrorist.'" *The Age of Terrorism*, 11.

46. Elshtain, *Just War Against Terror*, 57 and 80.

47. Khatchadourian, *The Morality of Terrorism*, 56.

48. Carr, *The Lessons of Terror*, 92–93.

49. For a summary of the historical, philosophical, and theological components of "Just War" theories and traditions, see my book with David Barash, *Peace and Conflict Studies*, 414–24.

50. Thucydides, *History of the Peloponnesian War*, Book 5, cited in Jonathan Glover, *Humanity A Moral History of the Twentieth Century* (New Haven: Yale University Press, 2000), 28–29. See also Michael Walzer's interpretation of the Melian Dialogue in *Just and Unjust Wars*, 5–13.

51. See Barash and Webel, *Peace and Conflict Studies*, 416–20.

52. For sieges and blockades, see Walzer, *Just and Unjust Wars*, chapter 10, 160–75. According to the military historian Sven Lindquist, "total war was an expression that began to be used in France during the First World War. … The most famous use was in *Der Totale Krieg* (*Total War*) the title of a book by General Erich Ludendorff. Modern war is total in the sense that it touches the lives and souls of every single civilian of the warring countries. Air bombardment has intensified the concept, since the entire area of the warring country has become a theater of war. 'The total war is a struggle of life or death and therefore has an ethical justification that the limited war of the 19th century lacked,' writes Ludendorff." Lindquist has provided the best extant chronicle and implicit critique of bombing and of how historically what had been "impermissible" in war (such as killing noncombatants) has gradually become "permissible," if certain "ethical justifications" are provided. Sven Lindquist, *A History of Bombing*, trans. Linda Haverty Rugg (New York: The New Press, 2001), 68.

53. Harrison Salisbury, *The 900 Days The Siege of Leningrad* (New York: Da Capo Press, 1981), 514–15. "More people had died in the Leningrad blockade than had ever died in a modern city—anywhere—anytime: more than ten times the number who died in Hiroshima. … A total for Leningrad and vicinity of something over 1,000,000 deaths attributable to hunger, and an over-all total of deaths, civilian and military, on the order of 1,300,000 to 1,500,000, seems reasonable…. *Pravda*…declared that 'the world has never known a similar mass extermination of a civilian

population, such depths of human suffering and deprivation as fell to the lot of Leningraders.' " In following chapters of this book, several stories of Leningraders ("babushki," or grandmothers) who survived the block-ade, will be told. They, and millions of other Russians, are still haunted by this worst siege in human history (so far...).

54. I have interviewed British and German officers who were on the sending and receiving ends of such bombings, and I discuss these cases in more detail in subsequent chapters.

55. Maurice Merleau-Ponty, *Humanism and Terror* (Boston: Beacon Press, 1969), 94.

56. Hannah Arendt, *On Violence* (Harcourt Brace & Company, Harvest Book: San Diego, 1970), 5.

57. See my book with David Barash, *Peace and Conflict Studies*, 58–64, for trends in warfare, especially in their frequency and lethality (increasingly for noncombatants); and "The Reasons for Wars," esp. 185–206, for the dominant role of the nation-state in modern warfare.

58. See Joel Kovel, *Against the State of Nuclear Terror* (Boston: South End Press, 1983); Gregg Herken, *The Winning Weapon: The Atomic Bomb in the Cold War 1945–1950* (Princeton: Princeton University Press, 1988); Jonathan Schell, *The Fate of the Earth* (New York: Knopf, 1982); and Robert Jay Lifton and Richard Falk, *Indefensible Weapons: The Political and Psychological Case Against Nuclearism* (New York: Basic Books, 1982).

59. See Barash and Webel, *Peace and Conflict Studies*, 87–93.

60. "Allegedly," because on the many occasions the "Cold" War was per-ilously close to being "hot," and not just during the Cuban Missile (or missive?) Crisis of October 1962. For a sophisticated analysis of the U.S. nuclear brinkmanship, see Michio Kaku and Daniel Axelrod, *To Win a Nuclear War: The Pentagon's Secret War Plans* (Boston: South End Press, 1987), esp. x–xi and 5.

61. "By nuclearism we mean psychological, political, and military depend-ence on nuclear weapons, the embrace of weapons as a solution to a wide variety of human dilemmas, most ironically that of 'security.' " Lifton and Falk, *Indefensible Weapons* ix. Also see Robert jay Lifton, *Superpower Syndrome: America's Apocalyptic Confrontation with the World* (New York: Thunder's Mouth Press/Nation Books, 2003).

62. Barash and Webel, 100–10.

63. See Silke, *Terrorists, Victims and Society* esp. part I ("The Terrorists") for a realistic portrait of who "terrorists" are, the reasons for their actions, the impact of terrorist violence on its victims, and some scenarios for deterring and responding to terrorism.

64. Ibid., 80–83.

65. Jimmy Carter, cited in Blum, *Rogue State,* unnumbered introductory page, originally cited in *The New York Times,* March 26, 1989, 16.

66. Jean Baudrillard, *The Spirit of Terrorism*, trans. Chris Turner (New York and London: Verso Books, 2002), 15 and 31.

3 Articulating the Ineffable:
The voices of the Terrified

1. "DUG ," interview by author, Amsterdam, Netherlands, May 9, 2003. "DUG" is the name assigned to the seventh (or "G," alphabetical order starting with A as the first) Dutch (or "DU") person interviewed. No interviews were recorded, and each interviewee was assured that his or her anonymity would be preserved.

2. Judith Herman, *Trauma and Recovery* (New York: Basic Books, 1997), 1, 33.

3. "SPB" was the second Spanish person interviewed, by the author with an interpreter, Madrid, Spain, December, 2, 2003. Like two other Spanish people I interviewed, "SFB" gave me a copy of her own (published) account of the attack. The publication of the memoirs/testimonies of victims of terrorism (both from below—as in Spain—and from above, as in Latin America) is a phenomenon distinctive of the Spanish-speaking world, as is the existence of numerous other books on terror and terrorism.

4. "SPB," interview.

5. Ibid.

6. Ibid. ETA is the acronym (Euskadi at Askatasuna, or Freedom for the Basque Homeland) of a militant Basque separatist group that often uses attacks on Spanish and Basque government officials (and civilians) as a means, so far unsuccessful, for compelling the Spanish government to grant independence to the Basque region of Spain. For ETA's similarities to and differences from other ethno-nationalist/separatist "terrorist" groups, see Bruce Hoffman, *Inside Terrorism*, 26–27, 45–65, 158–75, 197, and 206.

7. *Diagnostic and Statistical Manual of Mental Disorders, Fourth Edition, Text Revision (DSM-IV-TR)*, Washington, DC: American Psychiatric Association, 2002), 463–64.

8. Phenomenology is a systematic, originally philosophical, approach for describing the lived experiences of embodied human beings in this world. It was initiated (as "pure, transcendental, descriptive," and/or "genetic phenomenology") by the German philosopher Edmund Husserl during the early twentieth century, and was further developed (as "existential phenomenology") by his student Martin Heidegger and by the French philosophers Jean-Paul Sartre and Maurice Merleau-Ponty. Phenomenology has been "applied" to a wide range of fields in the human sciences, especially to psychology, psychiatry, and psychotherapy (by Rollo May, among others). Husserl's writings are notoriously difficult, but not entirely incomprehensible. See, e.g., *The Essential Husserl Basic Writings in Transcendental Phenomenology*, ed. Don Welton (Bloomington and Indianapolis: Indiana University Press, 1999). Merleau-Ponty states that "phenomenology can be practiced and identified as a manner or style of thinking, that existed as a movement before arriving at complete awareness of itself as a philosophy. ... We

shall find in ourselves, and nowhere else, the unity and true meaning of phenomenology. ... is accessible only through a phenomenological method...to be a 'descriptive psychology'. ... The whole universe of science is built upon the world as directly experienced ... we must begin by reawakening the basic experience of the world." Maurice Merleau-Ponty, *The Phenomenology of Perception* (London and New York: Routledge, 2002), viii–ix. For psychological applications of philosophical phenomenology, see Rollo May, Ernest Angel, and Henri F. Ellenberger, eds., *Existence A New Dimension in Psychiatry and Psychology* (New York: Simon and Schuster Clarion Books, 1958); Amedeo Giorgi, ed., *Phenomenology and Psychological Research* (Pittsburgh: Duquesne University Press, 1985); and Steiner Kvale, *Interviews: An Introduction to Qualitative Research Interviewing* (Thousand Oaks and London: Sage Publications, 1996).

9. "SPA," interview by author, Madrid, Spain, December 1, 2003.

10. Ibid.

11. Ibid.

12. Ibid.

13. "SPC," interview by author with interpreter, Madrid, Spain, December 2, 2003.

14. Ibid.

15. Ibid.

16. "LA," interview by author with interpreter, rural Latvia, Saldus Region, August 15, 2002.

17. Ibid.

18. Ibid.

19. Ibid.

20. "RA," interview by author and interpreter, St. Petersburg, Russia, October 10, 2002.

21. "URB," interview by author and interpreter, Kiev, Ukraine, May 19, 2003.

22. "GULAG" is a Russian acronym for "*Glavnoe Upravlenie Lagerei,*" or "Main Camp Administration." It became synonymous with the entire Soviet forced-labor camp system. See Anne Applebaum, *Gulag A History* (New York: Doubleday, 2003), 50.

23. "URB," interview.

24. Ibid.

25. "GG," interview by author, Wolfsburg, Germany, May 13, 2003.

26. Ibid.

27. Ibid.

28. Ibid.

29. "DUC," interview by author, Rotterdam, Netherlands, May 6, 2003.

30. Ibid.

31. Ibid. For the history of bombing during war, see Sven Lindquist, *A History of Bombing,* trans. Linda Haverty Rugg (New York: The New

Press, 2001). For a comprehensive—and controversial—account of the allied bombing of Germany during World War II, see Jorg Fischer, *Der Brand Deutschland im Bombenkrieg 1940–45* (Munich: Propylaen Verlag, 2002). Also see W.G. Sebald, *On the Natural History of Destruction,* trans. Anthea Bell (New York: Random House, 2003), vii–104. For an ethical analysis of bombing in general, and of the allied bombings of Germany (where over 600,000 civilians died between 1940 and 1945 because of that bombing) and Japan, see Jonathan Glover, *Humanity A Moral History of the Twentieth Century* (New Haven: Yale University Press), 64–116.

32. "EA," phone interview by author, London/Leicester, England, October 15, 2002.

33. Ibid.

34. "ESA," phone interview by author, Sun City Center, Florida/Ottawa, Canada, December 15, 2003.

35. Ibid.

36. "CHA," phone interview by author, Sun City Center, Florida/Los Angeles, February 22, 2003.

37. Ibid.

38. Ibid.

39. Ibid.

40. "DUD," interview with author, Amsterdam, Netherlands, May 6, 2003. On the Holocaust, see Raul Hilberg's classic works *Perpetrators Victims Bystanders The Jewish Catastrophe* 1933–45 (New York: HarperPerennial, 1992), and *The Destruction of the European* Jews (New York: New Viewpoints, 1973), as well as Eric A. Johnson, *Nazi Terror The Gestapo, Jews, and Ordinary Germans* (New York: Basic Books, 2000)

41. "DUD," interview.

42. Ibid.

43. Ibid.

44. Ibid.

45. Ibid.

46. Ibid.

47. "DUG," interview with author, Amsterdam, Netherlands, May 8, 2003.

48. "GD," interview with author, Berlin, Germany, April 18, 2003.

49. Ibid.

50. "AF," interview with author, Sun City Center, Florida, December 12, 2003.

51. See Hilberg, *Perpetrators Victims Bystanders*, 45, and Eric A. Johnson, *Nazi Terror*, for details about the "concentration" (labor/death) camps, and the respective roles played by Germans and their supporters. For more details about the killers and killing, also see Christopher R. Browning, *Ordinary Men Reserve Police Battalion 101 and the Final Solution in Poland* (New York: HarperPerennial, 1998) and Daniel Jonah Goldhagen, *Hitler's Willing Executioners Ordinary Germans and the Holocaust* (New York: Vintage Books, 1997).

52. "AF," interview.
53. Ibid.
54. "RLA," interview by author with interpreter, Saldus, Latvia, August 15, 2002.
55. "EB, " phone interview by author, London, England, October 15, 2002.
56. Ibid.
57. "AC" phone interview by author, Sun City Center/New York City, February 23, 2003.
58. Ibid.
59. Ibid.
60. "AA," phone interview by author, Sun City Center/New York City, February 13, 2003.
61. Ibid.
62. Ibid.
63. Ibid.
64. Ibid.
65. Ibid.

4 Surviving the Undurable: Coping, and Failing to Cope with Terror

1. Ronnie Janoff-Bulman, *Shattered Assumptions Towards a New Psychology of Trauma* (New York: The Free Press, 1992), 4.
2. Maurice Merleau-Ponty, *Humanism and Terror* (Boston: Beacon Press, 1969), 94.
3. See Sigmund Freud, *The Problem of Anxiety,* trans. Henry Alden Bunker (New York: W. W. Norton & Company), 1963. Freud variously describes anxiety as an affective signal of danger (67, 86, and 108–113); as a cause of repression (39–41); as the central problem in the formation of neurosis, or unconscious psychological conflict between the Ego ("Das Ich," or "The I"), as the agency of repression, and the Id ("Das Es," or "The It"), or libidinal/aggressive psychic energy (85); as a biologically indispensable function for all higher organisms (71); as an efferent process (70); as the product of or the reaction to psychological helplessness (77, 82, and 114); as a reaction to the loss, absence of, or separation from, a love object, or to the absence or loss of the love of a loved object (67–84 and 115–18); as a response to situations that should have ceased to invoke it (91); as a signal for influencing the pleasure/pain mechanism (69); as the "cathetic energy" of unconscious impulses "converted" into anxiety (39–40 and 107–09); and, following Otto Rank, as a reaction to one's experience of birth (20, 67–77, 94–97, and 108). Freud also focuses on (and overstates?) "the fear of a threatened castration" as a motivating force behind many defensive, self-protective reactions to anxiety. According to Freud, castration anxiety plays a key role in the formation of many neurotic symptoms, which often arise to ward off the threat (38–40, 46, 58–66, 79–83, and 87–90). Freud also

distinguishes between "true anxiety" (*Realangst*)—regarding a "known danger"—and "neurotic anxiety—a conflicted reaction to an unknown, instinctual danger" (112–13). Finally, in the *Addenda* to *The Problem of Anxiety*, Freud links anxiety to trauma ("helplessness"): "The danger situation is the recognized, remembered, and anticipated situation of helplessness. Anxiety is the original reaction to helplessness in the traumatic situation" (especially during early childhood), "which is later reproduced as a call for help in the danger situation" (114–15). A prototypical example of such a (potentially?) traumatic (traumatizing?) situation is the infant's anxiety that arises when the mother is *perceived* as "missing," and therefore the young child's fear that the most loved (external) object may be permanently lost. "The initial cause of anxiety, which the ego itself introduced, is therefore loss of perception of the object, which becomes equated with loss of the object. ... Later on ... loss of love ... becomes a new and far more enduring danger and occasion for anxiety" (119). As we shall see, when a person feels existentially threatened ("basic" or "annihilation anxiety"), or feels that a person or thing to which they are deeply "attached" has been, is being, or may be taken from them ("separation anxiety"), while the initial reaction may be intense fear, or even terror, the initially anxiety-ridden person may *subsequently* respond in an enraged, aggressive, and violent way against the real or perceived "enemy" who has "attacked" and wounded their fragile ego. This was evident shortly after September 11, 2001, when many otherwise apparently sane and politically progressive Americans (mostly males) reacted furiously to the attacks and called for immediate action against the as-yet unknown attackers ("Bomb 'em! Nuke 'em!") Violent conflict in the external world is thus often preceded by emotional conflicts in the inner world.

4. The standard dictionary definitions of anxiety are: (1). "A state of being anxious or experiencing a strong or dominating blend of uncertainty, agitation or dread, and brooding fear about some contingency," and, (2). "an abnormal and overwhelming sense of apprehension and of fear often marked by such physical symptoms as tension, tremor, sweating, palpitations, and increased pulse." Furthermore, there is *existential* anxiety: "a state of mind that is deeply troubled or distressed; especially one that results from apparently being confronted with nothingness." *Webster's Third New International Dictionary of the English Language, Unabridged* (Springfield, MA: Merriam-Webster Inc. 1993), 97.

5. For a "history" and an existential–psychological interpretation of anxiety, see Rollo May, *The Meaning of Anxiety* (New York: Pocket Books, 1977), esp. 198–99, for a definition of "basic anxiety" (which is similar to Paul Tillich's notion of "the threat of non-being," as well as to the "annihilation anxiety" emphasized in the work of the prominent psychoanalyst Melanie Klein and many of her "object-relations" followers). For recent psychiatric thinking about the etiology, diagnosis, and treatment of anxiety disorder(s), see Laszlo A. Papp and Jack M. Gorman, "Generalized

Anxiety Disorder," in Harold I. Kaplan and Benjamin J. Sadock, eds., *Comprehensive Textbook of Psychiatry/VI, Sixth Edition, Volume 1* (Baltimore: Williams & Wilkins, 1995), 1,236–249. Also see the *Diagnostic and Statistical Manual of Mental Disorders, Fourth Edition, Text Revision,* 429–484, "Anxiety Disorders," under which are included panic attacks, specific phobias, generalized anxiety disorder, PTSD, and obsessive-compulsive disorder, to which I shall return later in this chapter.

6. Melanie Klein, perhaps the most influential psychoanalytic theorist after Freud, focuses on the central role of "the death instinct" and the fear of annihilation, both in the psychic life of the infant, and more generally: "I hold that anxiety arises from the operation of the death instinct within the organism, is felt as fear of annihilation (death) and takes the form of the fear of persecution. The fear of the destructive impulse seems to attach itself at once to an object—or rather is experienced as the fear of an uncontrollable, overpowering object. Other important sources of primary anxiety are the trauma of birth (separation anxiety) and frustration of bodily needs; and these experiences are from the beginning [of human life] felt as being caused by objects." Melanie Klein, "Notes on Some Schizoid Mechanisms" (1946), in Juliet Mitchell, ed., *The Selected Melanie Klein* (New York: The Free Press, 1987), 179.

7. "Internal breach..," Chris R. Brewin, *Posttraumatic Stress Disorder Malady or Myth?* (New Haven: Yale University Press, 2003), 5; "the predominant emotional..," Janoff-Bulman, *Shattered Assumptions,* 64.

8. Stress and trauma exist on a continuum. According to the *Diagnostic and Statistical Manual of Mental Disorders, Fourth Edition, Text Revision,* 469, "if the disturbance (with such symptoms as 'a subjective sense of numbing, detachment, or absence of emotional responsiveness; a reduction in awareness of his or her surroundings; derealization; depersonalization or dissociative amnesia;...persistently reexperienced trauma;...and marked symptoms of anxiety...) lasts for a minimum of 2 days and a maximum of 4 weeks after the traumatic event,' it is called "Acute Stress Disorder". But "if symptoms persist beyond 4 weeks, the diagnosis of Posttraumatic Stress Disorder may be applied."

9. *Webster's Third New International Dictionary of the English Language Unabridged,* 2,432. Note that the first meaning stresses the *physical* dimension of trauma.

10. Sigmund Freud, "Beyond the Pleasure Principle," in Peter Gay, ed. *The Freud Reader* (New York: W.W. Norton & Company, 1995), 598 and 607.

11. Skeptics about the prevalence and utility of PTSD include the psychiatrist Sally Satel and the literary critic Frederick Crews—who view PTSD as "needlessly hyped" by antiwar activists (such as the eminent psychiatrist Robert J. Lifton) or as "pseudo-scientifically" extended to cover "repressed," and/or "recovered memories." See Felicia Lee, "Is Trauma Being Trivialized?" *The New York Times,* September 6, 2003, A13, A15; Sally Satel, "Returning from Iraq, Still Fighting Vietnam," *The New York*

Times, March 5, 2004, A23; and Frederick Crews, "The Trauma Trap," *The New York Review of Books,* March 11, 2004, 37–40. My emphasis in this book is not on entering the fray regarding "the memory wars" (if it were a debate about Melanie Klein's controversial claims about early childhood, it might be called "the mammary wars ... "), but on identifying possible linkages between extremely frightening (terrifying) experiences of people during wartime and terrorist attacks and the subsequent degree of trauma in these terror victims. For my purposes, the best book on trauma, terror, and PTSD is Herman's, *Trauma and Recovery,* a masterly account of "the dialectic of trauma" involving "terror, rage, and hatred of the traumatic moment" (50). Also indispensable is Janoff-Bulman's, *Shattered Assumptions.* For PTSD, its systematizers, historians, and skeptics, see John P. Wilson, Matthew J. Friedman, and Jacob D. Lindy, eds., *Treating Psychological Trauma and PTSD* (New York: The Guilford Press, 2001); Marion F. Solomon and Daniel J. Siegel, *Healing Trauma* (New York: W.W. Norton & Company, 2003); Brewin, *Posttraumatic Stress Disorder;* and Richard J. McNally, *Remembering Trauma* (Cambridge, MA: The Belknap Press of Harvard University Press, 2003).

12. Brewin, *Posttraumatic Stress Disorder,* 8. According to the *Diagnostic and Statistical Manual of Mental Disorders Fourth Edition Text Revision,* 466, the "lifetime prevalence for Posttraumatic Stress Disorder" is "approximately 8% of the adult population of the United States. ... Studies of at-risk individuals...yield variable findings, with the highest rates (ranging from between one-third and more than half of those exposed) found among survivors of rape, military combat and captivity, and ethnically or politically motivated internment and genocide." The latter rates are certainly consistent with my own findings, and while a lifetime reported prevalence (all cases) for PTSD of 8 percent of American adults may not appear dramatic—and may understate considerably the true prevalence of PTSD—it is significantly higher than the lifetime prevalence of most other psychological disorders, and would mean that over 20 million Americans will suffer from PTSD during their lives. For prevalence rates of PTSD victims in other cultures, see Robert Desjarlais, Leon Eisenberg, Byron Good, and Arthur Kleinman, *World Mental Health Problems and Priorities in Low-Income Countries* (New York: Oxford University Press, 1995), 46–50.

13. Derek Summerfield states that (as of 1998) "there have an estimated 160 wars and armed conflicts in the Third World since 1945, with 22 million deaths and 3 times as many injured....Torture is routine in over 90 countries. Of all casualties in World War I, 5 percent were civilians, in World War II 50 percent, over 80 percent in the US war in Vietnam, and currently over 90 percent." In the ongoing "war" between terrorists from below and from above, a 90–percent civilian casualty rate would be a low estimate. See Derek Summerfield, "The Social Experience of War

and Some Issues for the Humanitarian Field," in Patrick J. Bracken and Celia Petty, eds., *Rethinking the Trauma of War* (London and New York: Free Association Books, 1998), 9. For more information about the relative (to military deaths) and absolute (approximately 35 million in World War II) increase in civilian deaths, as well as historical trends in war, see Barash and Webel, *Peace and Conflict Studies,* 59–77.

14 For example, "GB," a semi-retired German American woman professor whom I interviewed in person on March 20, 2002, in Berkeley, California, recalls that "horrible bombing is something that never heals. It cannot heal. ... It's hard to accept that you're not safe, and you never knew which bomb would find you. ... *So you numb yourself because it's so horrible when you think about it.* ... You become apprehensive about little things. It would drive you crazy. ... The noise was like a wailing scream. ... You knew all the time you could be injured or killed. This never left your mind, and you never knew if you'd see your family again. ... It was insane." GB endured four years of bombing (1941–45) in the center of Berlin, where she worked in the Propaganda Ministry of Dr. Göbbels.

15. For the concept of a spectrum of PTSD, see John P. Wilson, Matthew J. Friedman, and Jacob D. Lindy, "Treatment Goals for PTSD," in Wilson, Friedman, and Lindy, eds., *Treating Psychological Trauma and PTSD,* 8. For the idea, initially proposed by L. Gilkerson, that trauma "should be defined in relation to a continuum of arousal and emergency responses ... (and) entails ... a further escalation of the [arousal of the nervous system and increase of adrenaline and cortical] system toward a kind of dramatically hyperaroused state in which the organism's ability effectively to respond to the threat begins to break down. The threat is too massive, too immediate, too 'unthinkable' in its proportions and implications to be encompassed by the organism's behavior responses." Susan Coates, "Introduction Trauma and Human Bonds," in Susan W. Coates, Jane L. Rosenthal, and Daniel S. Schechter, *September 11: Trauma and Human Bonds* (Hillsdale, NJ: The Analytic Press, 2003), 2–3. Coates et al. tend to focus on the *relational and attachment* issues involved in trauma, an emphasis congruent with much current thinking in psychoanalysis.

16. I conducted 49 of the 52 interviews: 17 in person without an interpreter; 18 in person with an interpreter; and 14 on the phone without an interpreter. Three interviews—two in Japan, one with a survivor of the Tokyo firebombing by the U.S. air force at the end of World War II and one with a "hibakusha" (an atomic-bomb survivor from Nagasaki), and one in Madrid with a survivor of a terrorist attack—were conducted without me by interpreter/interviewers whom I had trained. In chapter 2, I have included only interviews I myself conducted, with or without a interpreter. For data analysis purposes, I generally have included all interviews, except in specific cases where some data obtained were either

unreliable (as with "LB," a Latvian man who said he "volunteered" to serve with the SS but whose responses were inconsistent) and/or incomplete (as with "JB," a Japanese man who was in Tokyo during the air raids but who prematurely ended the interview with the interpreter).

17. The nations represented (with the number and gender of people interviewed from that country) are: Germany (8: 6 females and 2 males); the Netherlands (7: 5 females and 2 males); the United States (7: 6 males and 1 female); Spain (4: 3 females and 1 male); England (4: 2 females and 2 males); Latvia (4: 3 males and one female); Ukraine (4: 2 females and 2 males); Russia (3: 3 females); Japan (2: 2 males); Serbia/Yugoslavia (1 female); the Czech Republic (1 female); Denmark (1 male); Chile (1 male); and El Salvador (1 female). In addition, there were 4 Russian-Latvians (2 females and 2 males) who were interviewed. Although I made repeated and strenuous efforts both to increase the sample size and diversity—by attempting to include terror survivors from Africa, the Middle East, Asia, and other Latin American and European countries where terrorism, either from below or from above, has occurred—for various reasons I was unsuccessful. I was compelled, therefore, to rely mainly on social networks to find appropriate people to interview. Hence, the population described in this book is closer to a "convenience sample" than to a "statistically representative" sample of the population (TFB and TFA survivors) I am describing.

18 Chris Hedges, *War is a Force that Gives Us Meaning* (New York: Public Affairs, 2002), 164. Hedges was citing Dave Grossman's book *On Killing: The Psychological Cost of Learning to Kill in War and Society* (Boston: Little, Brown, 1996), 43–44.

19. "LVB," interview by author and interpreter, rural Latvia, August 14, 2002.

20. "CZA," interview by author and interpreter, Prague, Czech Republic, November 4, 2002. This lady also said "War is a power struggle, about money, and is cruel. Is killing the only way to deal with men who need the consent of the people to sell us out?"

21. For example, "RB," a Russian lady living in St. Petersburg, reported sometimes having flashbacks while watching war movies and having nightmares if she sees something that reminds her of her (dead) family. "GG," the German lady from Dresden who still venerates Hitler, mentioned how she "starts crying when she watches TV shows about the war." And "UB," Ukrainian woman born in 1916 whom I interviewed with an interpreter in Kiev on August 15, 2002, described her constant nightmares and flashbacks, induced by seeing films, when "I was reminded [of the war] and had to leave the movies not knowing whether it was real or a dream."

22. "JB," a Japanese "Hibakusha" (atomic-bomb survivor) who was born in 1929, was interviewed in person on July 1, 2003 in Tokyo by an interpreter I had trained. The interpreter reports JB as having said, "When I

saw the mushroom-looking cloud, I thought that it is a volcano." JB then drew a picture of the mushroom-like atomic-bomb cloud. In Nagasaki, JB also "saw thousands of dead and wounded. You had to burn the dead. But there was no gasoline to help burn the corpses—the bodies did not burn very well. The grease of dead bodies burns longer." (JB reportedly gave a little laugh as he said this.)

23. "GF," a retired German male professor I interviewed in Heidelberg on April 11, 2003, noted that, although he saw very little combat, he had dreams of being strafed by allied forces more than 30 years after the end of World War II. He was also in a POW camp in the south of England, where he "almost starved to death." He cried during some of the interview, especially when recalling his dead father and wife, as well as Dachau (which he said he know about) and the extermination camps (such as Auschwitz), which he said he "didn't know about but was afraid might exist." Like all the Germans I interviewed, except one, he blamed Hitler and the Nazis for the war.

24. "DUA," interview by author and interpreter, Amsterdam, Netherlands, October 16, 2002. She was later interned in Westerbork and Theresienstadt, but she and her entire family survived the war and Holocaust, "a real miracle," in her words.

25. "RB," interview by author and interpreter, St. Petersburg, Russia, October 10, 2002.

26. "AA," the young American woman who was in midtown Manhattan, instead of in her regular office near the WTC, on September 11, 2001, recalled how "she started to smell the smoke, like burning oil, which was horrible, and the air had changed....I couldn't breathe, because the smell was so bad." "AA," interview by author.

27. Freud, "Thoughts on War and Death" (1915), in *Collected Papers, Volume 4*, 304–305.

28. Ernest Becker, *The Denial of Death* (New York: The Free Press, 1973), 15; also see Sherwin B. Nuland, *How We Die Reflections on Life's Final Chapter* (New York: Alfred A. Knopf, 1994), who says, "as with every other looming terror and looming temptation, we seek ways to deny the power of death and the icy hold in which it grips human thought," xv; and Elisabeth Kubler-Ross, *On Death and Dying* (New York: Touchstone Books, 1969).

29. Sigmund Freud, "Psychoanalysis and Trauma Neuroses" (1919), in *Collected Papers, Volume 5*, 86–87.

30. PTSD is not like a viral or bacterial infection, with globally accepted and quantitative scientific tests to measure precisely the pathogenesis of the disease in an organism. I relied on a qualitative, semi-structured interview protocol consisting of 27 questions, 8 of which are designed to obtain biographical information, 14 of which tap interviewees' recollections of and reactions to their experiences of political terror, and 5 of which are open-ended. I also employed my "clinical intuition," derived

from years of psychoanalytic and psychotherapeutic training and experience, to assess the interviewee's verbal (self-reports) and nonverbal (body language and related observable markers) degree of terror during the attack (on a 1 to 5 scale, with 1 the lowest, 3 moderate, and 5 the highest), and level of current PTSD. Those who rated 1 or 2 on both the terror and PTSD scales are considered "low" in terror and PTSD, and those who scored 4–5 on both the terror and PTSD scales are considered "high" in their exposure to terror and current manifestation of PTSD.

31. This is "common sense" and "popular wisdom," according to Ronnie Janoff-Bulman, who, in *Shattered Assumptions*, 87–88, states: "Popular wisdom suggests that those who have the greatest psychological problems prior to a victimization will have a particularly difficult time in the aftermath of a traumatic event....Those who are extremely anxious or depressed before a victimization are apt to look even more troubled after being victimized. In the well-established psychiatric vulnerability model, prior stressors and psychological history predispose people to further problems. Research has, in fact, shown that preexisting problems are associated with chronic psychological symptomatology postvictimization."

32. For "obsessive-compulsive" and "narcissistic" "character types" and "personality disorders," see the *Diagnostic and Statistical Manual of Mental Disorders Fourth Edition Text Revision*, 725–729 for "Obsessive-Compulsive Personality Disorder," and 714–717 for "Narcissistic Personality Disorder." Also see Wilhelm Reich, *Character Analysis, Third, Enlarged Edition*, trans. Vincent R. Carfagno (New York: Farrar, Straus and Giroux, 1983), esp. 209–224; Otto Kernberg, *Borderline Conditions and Pathological Narcissism* (New York: Jason Aronson, Inc., 1975), esp. 227–243 and 315–327, for a useful discussion of the differences between "normal" and "pathological" narcissism"; and Ian Osborn, *Tormenting Thoughts and Secret Rituals The Hidden Epidemic of Obsessive-Compulsive Disorder* (New York: Dell Trade Paperback, 1998), 6–7, for a view of "OCD" as a neurobiological, not a psychological, "disorder."

33. Sigmund Freud, "Libidinal Types," in *Collected Papers, Volume 5,* ed. James Strachey (New York: Basic Books, 1959), 249–250.

34. For an intellectual history of the concepts of self, ego, and narcissism, see Charles Webel, "Self: An Overview," in Benjamin Wolman, ed., *The International Encyclopedia of Psychiatry, Psychoanalysis, Psychology, and Neurology (Progress Volume)* (New York: Asclepius Press, 1983), 398–403. For a social critique of egocentrism and self-interest, see Charles Webel, "From Self-Knowledge to Self-Obsessed Self-Interest," *New Ideas in Psychology*, 14:3 (1996), 189–95.

35. See Juan E. Mezzich, Arthur Kleinman, Horacio Fabrega, and Delores L. Parron, *Culture and Psychiatric Diagnosis A DSM-IV Perspective* (Washington, DC: American Psychiatric Press, Inc., 1996), xvii–25.

36. See Anatol Rappaport, *The Origins of Violence: Approaches to the Study of Conflict* (New Brunswick, NJ: Transaction Publishers, 1997), esp. 73–94

"Uses and Limitations of the Psychological Approach," for an acute analysis of aggressiveness, personality theory, "cognitive dissonance," and "attitudinal balance. Also see David Barash and Charles Webel, *Peace and Conflict Studies,* part II: The Reasons for Wars, esp. 119–143. For the decisive role of perceived authority ("leadership") and group pressure to conform, see Stanley Milgram, *Obedience to Authority* (New York: Harper Colophon Books, 1975). Possibly the most famous, or infamous, experiment in the history of social psychology was conducted by Milgram with a group of Yale University students, 60% of whom were "fully obedient" to perceived authority, even when they (incorrectly) believed their actions resulted in extreme pain (electric shocks) and injury to their "victims." Similar experiments conducted in other, more "natural" settings, both in the United States and in other "industrialized democracies" *found that up to 85% of the subjects were absolutely obedient to perceived authorities.* As Milgram himself claims, "The results...are disturbing. They raise the possibility that human nature, or—more specifically—the kind of character produced in American democratic society, cannot be counted on to insulate its citizens from brutality and inhumane treatment at the direction of malevolent authority. A substantial proportion of people do what they are told to do, irrespective of the content of the act and the limitations of their conscience, so long as they perceive that the command comes from a legitimate authority," *Obedience to Authority,* 188–89. Moreover, my research seems to indicate that the vast majority of people comply with orders they may even perceive as "immoral and unjustified" in order to maintain social cohesion, to maximize personal self-interest, and to promote individual and familial survival. Despite often considerable psychophysiological tension and moral conflict, skilled survivors adapt to whatever environment in which they find themselves. Most political leaders and others who give orders (e.g. to kill the "enemy"), and the overwhelming majority of the soldiers and civilians who comply with such demands, are neither "good nor evil," but are motivated primarily by their (partially) socially constructed "need for self-preservation," irrespective of the damage done to others (preferably unseen and unheard).

37. "The most relevant heredity-based characteristic for goodness and evil seems to be temperament." Ervin Staub, *The Psychology of Good and Evil: Why Children, Adults, and Groups Help and Harm Others* (New York: Cambridge University Press, 2003), 13.

38. I presented the data about Hispanic vulnerability to terror and trauma to several colleagues. One, a female social psychologist (half Puerto-Rican), stressed the possible cultural and social factors. Another, a male artist from Colombia, thought that insecure and nervous mothers, especially recent Latin American immigrants living without male providers in New York City, transmit their fears and anxieties to their children. And the third, a male anesthesiologist, said "of course." I asked him why, and he replied that he had spent decades in emergency and operating rooms

watching people being born and dying. He observed that "they" (Hispanics) "come into the world screaming and go out screaming." The implication is that Hispanics are "hardwired" (brains, nervous systems, genes ...) in a way that makes them more susceptible to trauma than other ethnic groups....Obviously, much more research is needed.

39. In her otherwise remarkably perceptive book *Trauma and Recovery*, Judith Herman asserts that "The most powerful determinant of psychological harm is the character of the traumatic event itself. Individual personality characteristics count for little in the face of overwhelming events," 57. But on the very next page, she backtracks: "The impact of traumatic events also depends on the resilience of the afflicted person. While studies of combat veterans in the Second World War have shown that every man has his 'breaking point,' some 'broke' more easily than others." Exactly. My study indicates that *all* combat veterans I interviewed "broke" at some point, and they remain, to a greater or lesser degree, "broken." While "the character of the traumatic event" is of considerable importance, it does not appear to be *as* important as "individual personality characteristics" in determining who and when someone "breaks" or does not "break." Many of the people I interviewed were exposed to roughly the same (potentially) traumatic events, and some "broke" (sooner or later) and others did not. A good example of this is the couple who were together all of September 11, 2001. The male ("AA") seems never to have "broken," whereas his partner ("EC") was deeply affected almost immediately, and is still shaken, more than two years after 9/11. Ronnie Janoff-Bulman, in *Shattered Assumptions*, 88–89, perhaps counterintuitively, argues that "it is those *with the most positive preexisting assumptions* whose core schemas are most deeply violated. Extreme negative events produce tremendous psychological upheaval and anxiety, for their inner worlds are shattered...[But] these survivors may have a relatively easy time rebuilding a stable, comfortable assumptive world, the essence of the recovery process." In other words, "optimists" may more easily be terrified and temporarily traumatized than others, but they are less prone to *chronic* trauma. And Bruno Bettelheim famously postulated "only three different psychological responses" to "the concentration camp experience.: one group allowed their experiences to destroy them; another tried to deny it any lasting impact; and a third engaged in a lifelong struggle to remain aware and to try to cope with most terrible, but nevertheless occasionally realized, dimensions of man's existence... *the concentration camp survivor syndrome*....A precondition for a new integration is acceptance of how severely one has been traumatized, and of what the nature of the trauma has been." Bruno Bettelheim, *Surviving and Other Essays* (New York: Alfred A. Knopf, 1979), 28, 34. My research indicates otherwise: the people I interviewed—including concentration camp survivors—who appeared best "integrated" after their terrifying experiences were

distinguishable from others who seem less "reintegrated" *by virtue of their denial and repression of acutely painful feelings and memories, not by explicit "acceptance" of their trauma.* Those who seemed most "accepting" of how they had been traumatized, seemed most stuck in their painful memories (often flashbacks) and emotions (anxiety, sadness, and anger). For useful discussions of coping, resiliency after a trauma (especially a potentially devastating personal loss), and treatment of the traumatized, see Mardi J. Horowitz, *Treatment of Stress Response Syndromes* (Washington, DC: American Psychiatric Publishing, Inc., 2003), and George A. Bonanno, "Loss, Trauma, and Human Resilience," *American Psychologist*, 59 (January 2004), 20–28; and Daniel B. Herman, Barbara Pape Aaron, and Ezra S. Susser, "An Agenda for Public Mental Health in a Time of Terror," in Coates et al., *September 11: Trauma and Human Bonds*, esp. 246–252 ("Treating the Trauma").

40. See Sheldon Solomon, Jeff Greenberg, and Tom Pyszczynski "Why War? Fear is the Mother of All Violence," in Stanley Krippner and Teresa M. McIntyre, eds., *The Psychological Impact of War Trauma on Civilians: An International* Perspective (Westport, CT: Praeger Publishers 2003), esp. 300–01, for the "human propensities that contribute to war," such as the "deep existential threat" posed by others perceived as "hostile" and constructed as "scapegoats" upon whom we project and direct our fears and hostilities in order to shield ourselves from our own anxieties. The filmmaker and author Michael Moore, in "Bowling for Columbine," also focuses on fear as a principal reason for Americans' obsessions with firearms and violence.

41. For the "basic instincts," especially fear and anxiety and their alleged source in the section of the brain called the amygdala, see Joseph LeDoux, *The Emotional Brain: The Mysterious Underpinnings of Emotional Life* (New York: Touchstone Books, 1998), 112–14; and *Synaptic Self: How Our Brains Become Who We Are* ((New York: Penguin Books, 2003), 214–25 and 282–95. Also see Antonio R. Damasio, *The Feeling of What Happens: Body and Emotion in the Making of Consciousness* (New York: Harcourt Brace & Company), 42–81, for the differences between emotions ("publicly observable") and feelings ("private mental"), especially fear; and *Looking for Spinoza Joy, Sorrow, and the Feeling Brain* (New York: Harcourt, Inc. 2003), 29–46, "The primary (or basic) emotions...fear, anger, disgust, surprise, sadness, and happiness...are easily definable in human beings across several cultures and in non-human species as well....most of what we know about the neurobiology of emotion comes from studying the primary emotions. Fear leads the way. ... " Damasio goes on to assess "the social emotions," including sympathy, same, pride, envy, gratitude, indignation and contempt. For my purposes, terror is acute fear, and rage is intense anger; *they are both "basic" and "social" emotions.* Moreover, Martha Nussbaum (following Wittgenstein and child analysis) claims that "the *earliest*

emotions are likely to be fear and anxiety," *Upheavals of Thought: The Intelligence of Emotions* (New York: Cambridge University Press, 2001), 190. But I and many others part ways from neuroscience when it attempts entirely to "reduce" and "identify" human mental life (consciousness) and affect (emotions and feelings) to brain states, and, moreover, further to identify psychopathology and mental illness (as well as ethics . . .) with "damaged" brain states. For a critique of this psychological materialism and reductionism see Charles Webel and Anthony Stigliano, "Are We 'Beyond Good and Evil?' Radical Psychological Materialism and the 'Cure' for Evil," *Theory & Psychology,* 14:1 (2004), 81–103.

42. *The Sayings of Confucius* (Torrance, CA: Heian International Publishing, 1983), 50.

43. Ibid., 16.

44. Freud, *Civilization and Its Discontents,* in *The Freud Reader,* ed. Peter Gay (New York: W. W. Norton & Company, 1995), 754–756. In *Why War?*—Freud's reply to a letter from Albert Einstein, Freud added, " . . . this (Death) instinct is at work in every living being and is striving to bring it to ruin and to reduce life to its original condition of inanimate matter. Thus it quite seriously deserves to be called a death instinct, while the erotic instincts represent the effort to live. The death instinct turns into the destructive instinct if, with the help of special organs, it is directed outwards, on to objects. The living creature preserves its own life . . . by destroying an extraneous one. Some portion of the death instinct, however, remains operative within the living being, and we have sought to trace quite a number of normal and pathological phenomena to this internalization of the destructive instinct." Sigmund Freud, *Collected Papers, Volume 5,* 282.

45. *Reich Speaks of Freud,* ed. Mary Higgins and Chester M. Raphael (New York: Farrar, Straus and Giroux, 1967), 89, passim.

46. Joan Riviere, following Melanie Klein, argues that "the concept of the destructive force within every individual, tending towards the annihilation of life, is naturally one which arouses extreme emotional resistances; and this, together with the inherent obscurity of its operation, have led to a marked neglect of it by many of Freud's followers." Joan Riviere, cited by Jacqueline Rose, *Why War?* (Cambridge, MA: Blackwell Publishers, 1993), 147–148.

47. Franco Fornari, *The Psychoanalysis of War,* trans. Alenka Pfeifer (Garden City, NY: Anchor Books, 1974), 52–53.

48. Erich Fromm, *The Anatomy of Human Destructiveness* (New York: Henry Holt and Company, 1992), 498–520, for a penetrating, yet sympathetic, critique of Freud's notion of a death instinct in particular, and of Freudian dualistic thinking in general.

49. " . . . war represents a social institution the aim of which is to cure paranoid and depressive anxieties existing . . . in every man. This organization serves two security functions. . . . The first part corresponds to the

defense against external danger (i.e., the real flesh-and-blood enemy), while the other, the hidden part, corresponds to an unconscious security maneuver against terrifying fantasy entities which are not flesh and blood but represent an absolute danger (as experienced, for example in nightmares) which we could call the 'Terrifier'....an internal, absolute enemy similar to a nightmare." The internal 'terrifier' then is unconsciously transformed "into an external, flesh-and-blood adversary who can be faced and killed," Fornari, *The Psychoanalysis of War*, xvi. While there are obvious limitations with any reductionist approach, especially a psychoanalytic one that claims to infer unconscious mental processes and agencies from the clinical interpretation of patients' dreams and associations, this kind of speculation is useful for examining the blind and ferocious intensity many warriors and political/military decision-makers bring to their hostilities.

CONCLUSION: IMAGINING THE UNIMAGINABLE? A WORLD WITHOUT (OR WITH LESS...) TERROR AND TERRORISM?

1. Marcus Aurelius, *Meditations,* H.1 and VI.6, cited in Martha C. Nussbaum, "Compassion and Terror," in *Daedalus,* (Winter 2003), 21.
2. *The Gospel According to Matthew,* 6, 38–39, 43–44, and 46, in *The New Testament of the New American Bible, St. Joseph* Edition (New York: Catholic Book Publishing Co., 1986), 18.
3. *The Qur'an,* Surah 8, 60–61, trans. Abdullah Yusuf Ali (Elmhurst, NY: Tahrike Tarsile Qur'an, Inc., 2003), 112.
4. *The Essential Talmud,* Adin Steinsaltz, trans. Chaya Galai (New York: Basic Books, 1976), 204.
5. *The Dhammapada* (Sydney, Australia: Axiom Publishing, 2003), 7, 44, 65, and 81.
6. *Bhagavad-Gita, Commentary by Mahatma Gandhi* (Sydney, Australia: Axiom Publishing, 2002), 33 and 79.
7. *Gandhi on Nonviolence,* ed. Thomas Merton (New York: New Directions Publishing Corporation, 1965), 52.
8. Gandhi once said, "It is better to be violent, if there is violence in our breasts, than to put on the cloak of nonviolence to cover impotence. Violence is any day preferable to impotence. There is hope for a violent man to become nonviolent. There is no such hope for the impotent." M.K. Gandhi, cited in Jonathan Schell, *The Unconquerable World Power, Nonviolence, and the Will of the People* (New York: Metropolitan Books, 2003), 130.
9. Albert Einstein, "To Sigmund Freud," in *Ideas and Opinions,* trans. Sonja Bargmann (New York: Wings Books, not dated), 104.
10. Sigmund Freud, "Why War"? (1932), *Collected Papers,* Volume 5, 274, and 278.
11. Freud, ibid., 278.

12. Bernard Shaw, *Man and Superman* (New York: Penguin Books, 1957), 142, and 144.

13. The quintessential example of this polarizing, splitting mentality—"you're either with us" (the United States and its "coalition partners") "or you're with them" ("the terrorists")—is David From's and Richard Perle's screed, *An End to Evil How to Win the War Against Terror* (New York: Random House, 2003), which is not alone in omitting any analysis of either "evil" or of "terror," and instead proselytes for recruits to the "War on Terrorism." To help the United States win the "victory" over "evil/Terrorism," From and Perle make a number of reasonable recommendations regarding the safeguarding of North America's ports, nuclear plants, and other domestic facilities (in chapter 4, "The War at Home"), as well as the expectable injunction to "take the battle to our enemies," wherever they be, especially in the Middle East (in chapter 5, "The War Abroad"). For the acquiescent role played by the American mass media, see Edward S. Herman and Noam Chomsky, *Manufacturing Consent The Political Economy of the Mass Media* (New York: Pantheon Books, 2002); Noam Chomsky, *Media Control The Spectacular Achievements of Propaganda*, second edition (New York: Seven Stories Press, 2002); and Sheldon Rampton and John Stauber, *Weapons of Mass Deception The Uses of Propaganda in Bush's War on Iraq* (New York: Jeremy P. Tarcher/Penguin Books), 2003, esp. chapter 5, "The Uses of Fear," for the Bush II administration's spinning of "terrorism" as a "form of propaganda" to induce and manipulate the public to support its political/military/economic hegemonic agenda.

14. I was told by a historian at the Dutch Center for War Documentation in Amsterdam that some contemporary historians believe that the incendiary bombing of Rotterdam by the Luftwaffe was a "mistake," whereas other historians believe it was intended.

15. I was told by a Serbian psychologist in Belgrade that NATO's bombings neither forced the withdrawal of Serbian military and police forces from Kosovo, nor did any real damage to them. She claimed the Serb forces withdrew for internal political reasons, and what NATO in fact bombed were not Serb soldiers and weapons, but empty paper shacks and mock tanks. According to her, virtually all the people who were killed and injured by NATO's bombing were civilian noncombatants (and Chinese diplomats).

16. Susan Sontag (citing Simone Weil, "The Iliad, or The Poem of Force," 1940), *Regarding the Pain of Others* (New York: Farrar, Straus and Giroux, 2003), 12.

17. Khatchadourian, *The Morality of Terrorism*, p. xiii.

18. Karl Jaspers, *The Future of Mankind* (Chicago: The University of Chicago Press, 1967), 17.

19. Sigmund Freud, "Why War"?, *Collected Papers*, Volume 5, 287.

20. Noam Chomsky, *Hegemony or Survival America's Quest for Global Dominance* (New York: Metropolitan Books, 2003), 2.

21. Albert Einstein, "A Message to Intellectuals" (1948), *Ideas and Opinions*, 148.

22. Maurice Merleau-Ponty, *Humanism and Terror* (Boston: Beacon Press, 1969), xxxvi and xxxviii.

23. Albert Camus, *Neither Victims Nor Executioners*, trans. Dwight MacDonald (Chicago: World Without War Publishers, 1972), 25 and 55.

24. Aristotle, *Poetics* (1452), in *The Basic Works of Aristotle*, ed. Richard McKeon (New York: The Modern Library, 2001), 1464–465.

25. In *Regarding the Pain of Others*, 125–126, Susan Sontag has luminously portrayed the images of slaughtered Russian soldiers, who "are not about to yell at us to bring a halt to that abomination which is war. They haven't come back to life in order to stagger off to denounce the war-makers who sent them to kill and be killed. And they are not represented as terrifying to others. ... These dead are supremely uninterested in the living; in those who took their lives; in witnesses—and in us. ... We don't get it. We truly can't imagine what it was like. We can't imagine how dreadful, how terrifying war is; and how normal it becomes. ... That's what every soldier, and every journalist and aid worker and independent observer who has put in time under fire, and had the luck to elude the death that struck others nearby, stubbornly feels. And they are right." Some of the people I interviewed may be considered among "the living dead," because years, decades, after they survived the terrors of war they are still mesmerized, traumatized, paralyzed by what they saw (and in some cases, did). ... They have much to teach us. ...

26. For the "four major root causes of evil, or reasons that people act in ways that others will perceive as evil," especially the "simple desire for material gain, such as money or power.., threatened egotism," and "violent revenge," see Roy F. Baumeister, *Evil Inside Human Violence and Cruelty* (New York: Henry Holt & Company, 2001), 152–55 and 375–78.

27. According to Richard Falk, we may now be living in a "Gandhian moment": "At this time in human history, it would seem that ... the passions that rage on the planet suggest an impending encounter between those destructive forces that see the glass totally empty, and those that believe it is almost full; between the extremists, whether religious or secular, locked in total war, and the visionary warriors that constitute global civil society who believe in a future based on peace, justice, and sustainability. Looking back in time, we can understand that it is an error to be too literal in anticipating the Gandhian moment, but it would be a greater error to dismiss this possibility, and reconcile ourselves either to endless and escalating cycles of violence or to the 'unpeace' of injustice and oppression." Richard Falk, "A New Gandhian Moment," *TRANSCEND Bulletin*, www.transcend.org, March 11, 2004. Also see Richard Falk, *The Great Terror War* (New York: The Olive Branch Press, 2003). Notable publications by other "visionary warriors" include Gene Sharp, *The Politics of Nonviolent Action, Parts One, Two, and Three*

(Boston: Peter Sargent Publishers, 1973), and *Making Europe Unconquerable The Potential of Civilian-Based Deterrence and Defense* (Cambridge, MA: Ballinger Publishing Company, 1986); Joan V. Bondurant, *Conquest of Violence The Gandhian Philosophy of Conflict* (Princeton: Princeton University Press, 1988); *The Power of Nonviolence Writings by Advocates of Peace* (Boston: Beacon Press, 2002); Michael Nagler, *Is There No Other Way? The Search for a Nonviolent Future* (Berkeley: Berkeley Hills Books, 2001); Elise Boulding, *Cultures of Peace The Hidden Side of History* (Syracuse: Syracuse University Press, 2000); Marrack Goulding, *Peacemonger* (Baltimore: The Johns Hopkins University Press, 2003); Jonathan Schell, *The Unconquerable World Power, Nonviolence, and the Will of the People* (New York: Metropolitan Books, 2003); and Barash and Webel, *Peace and Conflict Studies*, chapters 1, 2, and 10–21. Nonlethal means of subduing violent individuals and unruly crowds (such as nontoxic gases and nonintrusive tasers and stun-guns) have been around for a long time. If Departments of Defense would devote, say, 5 percent of their research and development funds to testing and deploying nonviolent and nonlethal implements of behavioral management, many lives and egos might be preserved.

28. Caleb Carr advises that "Assassination of rebel leaders, it will be remembered, was one of the most effective Roman policies for quelling uprisings, far more effective than large-scale punitive war" (though Rome itself was eventually invaded and overthrown by rebel leaders from the far north of the empire). Carr continues, "Today, we should bear that lesson in mind and remember that terror's only effective, legitimate use is against military personnel and against heads of state (the latter becoming, in times of war, supreme commanders, and therefore military as well as civilian leaders)." Caleb Carr, *The Lessons of Terror* (New York: Random House, 2002), 251. The logic of this position, however, would lead to the conclusion that Al Qaeda and other terrorist groups, from their point of view, would also be "justified" in targeting U.S.-led coalition members' "military personnel and heads of state." The assassination and terror game can be played by every side participating in it....

29. Vladimir Putin, cited in *The New York Times*, "Bombing of Subway in Moscow Kills 39 at Rush Hour," February 7, 2004, A5.

30. See Susan Sachs, "Poll Finds Hostility Hardening Toward U.S. Policies," *The New York Times*, March 17, 2004, A3.

INDEX